Developing an
Effective School Staff
Evaluation Program

Developing an
Effective School Staff
Evaluation Program

Jerry J. Herman

Parker Publishing Company, Inc.   West Nyack, N.Y.

Library of Congress Cataloging in Publication Data

Herman, Jerry John, (date)
    Developing an effective school staff evaluation
program.

    Bibliography: p.
    1. Teachers, Rating of. 2. School employees,
Rating of. I. Title.
LB2838.H4   371.1'44   72-7278
ISBN 0-13-204149-9

Staff Evaluation As a Key to Accountability

The educational institutions of this nation are besieged by internal and external forces demanding that these institutions be held accountable. Taxpayers are making statements such as "Don't ask us for additional money until you prove to us that you are using wisely what we now give you." Board members with management orientations are making statements similar to "Provide us with cost benefit breakdowns on existing programs before we will approve costly expansions of programs." Parents are asking "What are you teaching our children and why?" Teachers' unions and associations are continually saying such things as "We can do it better than the traditional way and the board and the administration should allow us to decide educational matters." Restated, these questions of accountability might well read: What are you doing? Who is responsible for doing it? What does it cost? Are there better ways of doing it in terms of effectiveness and cost? And how are you going to prove to us that we are getting our money's worth?

One of the most basic elements in accountability is staff evaluation. This element deals with definitions of what we are doing, who is responsible for doing it, and how do we measure the program effectiveness and the effectiveness of the work assigned each individual within the program. In other words: *Who is Accountable for What?*

Within the basic area of staff accountability, there are many questions asked that have, for the most part, gone unanswered. Some of the typical questions in need of answers are as follows:

5

Have you experienced frustration when a teacher has told you: "I know I'm weak in this area; will you help me to improve?" What have you answered when someone asks: "You always say that we have a good staff, but can you prove it to me?" Have you had guilt feelings when you ask for additional staff or money for in-service and you cannot really give a detailed, defensive answer as to the need? Have you ever been frustrated when questioned about your recommendations for funded programs or for tenure appointments or for promotional appointments? If you can answer "yes" to these and many other similar questions, then *you* are the person for whom this book is written.

As a practicing administrator, I am aware of the need for sound answers to such questions as those previously asked. During many years as a teacher, elementary principal, elementary curriculum coordinator, secondary curriculum coordinator, research coordinator, assistant superintendent for instruction and superintendent of schools, I have witnessed the need for and tackled the problems of staff evaluation from many angles. Several key factors have emerged: (1) We have often neglected to tell an employee what, specifically, is his job (detailed job descriptions); and, therefore, we are unfair when we hold him responsible for assignments of which he is unaware. (2) We often forget to meet with the employee to identify what is to be achieved (performance goals). (3) We frequently do not state goals in terms which can be measured for evaluative purposes (behavioral objectives), and, (4) Once we point out a weakness in an employee's performance, we often do not take the responsibility of assisting him in the elimination of the weakness (in-service and job upgrading) . . . and in consistent follow-up to insure improvement.

This book offers practical, realistic and usable suggestions on staff evaluation, in a concise manner so the busy administrator will be able to quickly locate needed information. Sufficient depth is included so as to give detailed help to administrators who have the responsibility for staff evaluations.

The contents provide practical details of the evaluative process as well as pinpointing the where, when, why, what, who, and how, of evaluating teachers, administrators, custodians, secretaries, food service personnel and other staff positions. Emphasis is placed on follow-up procedures. Once the evaluations are completed and weaknesses located, the evaluator must provide appropriate assistance in overcoming the weaknesses that have been discovered. Specific follow-up procedures are detailed in a manner that allows the reader a choice of practical suggestions.

The book is organized so that a broad variety of effective procedures and methods is presented, and sample materials will demonstrate how the procedures and methods can be effectively applied to your needs. Finally, this book emphasizes that accountability can only take place through people. Staff accountability is the initial building block in a total program of accountability for educational institutions.

Jerry J. Herman

CONTENTS

One

ESTABLISHING
THE FRAMEWORK
FOR STAFF EVALUATION

The evaluation program that is finally developed by any local school district is dependent upon proper planning. Ideally, the individuals given the overall responsibility for development should be representative of those persons who are to be evaluated and those individuals who are to actually do the evaluation.

Once the team members who are to be given the responsibility for developing the framework for staff evaluation are selected, they must arrive at a local definition of the term evaluation. In arriving at the local definition of the term evaluation, the initial dimensions of the task must be related to:

1. Sizing up the need.
2. Developing the rationale to guide program development.
3. Determining the necessary decisions as to *who* evaluates, *what* is to be evaluated, *why* evaluation is needed, *when* evaluation is to take -place, *where* evaluation shall be conducted and *how* the evaluative scheme that is ultimately developed shall be fitted into the existing operational structure.

The gestalt of evaluation involves the interweaving of diagnostic concerns, measurement techniques and prescriptive behaviors—each of these interlaced in a cyclical manner that provides for continuous modification of the total framework. Figure 1-1 provides a diagramatic representation of this process.

SIZING UP THE NEED

In determining the degree of need for a total staff evaluation program, one should begin by assessing what is being done and the degree to which current practice is satisfactory. Such key considerations as the following need be considered: (1) Is there a meaningful program for the selection of various categories of staff to be employed? (2) Does the staff specifically know what is expected of them? (3) Is there consensus on the purpose of evaluation? (4) Is there consensus on the methodology of evaluation? (5) Is there planned positive use in staff development of the informations gained from evaluation? and (6) Is there a felt need that evaluation is desirable and/or that the current evaluative program can be improved? If the investigation of these key considerations reveals weaknesses that need correction, the committee investigating evaluation needs and procedures is over its initial hurdle, and it can begin to investigate the formulation of a district-wide scheme of improvement.

DEVELOPING A RATIONALE

The mechanics of initiating evaluative program development can take many forms. It can be superimposed upon the staff by an unilateral decision of the board of education or the superintendent of schools, a program can be developed by the total administrative staff or a selected group of representative administrators and then placed into operation with or without in-service. It can be done by an outside expert or agency, or an evaluative program can be developed and implemented by involving a representative sampling of all staff categories or by total staff involvement. Of course, any combination of the above plans may be utilized by a specific school district; and there are advantages and disadvantages to any of the methods proposed.

EVALUATION: An Interlocking Diagnostic-Prescriptive Process

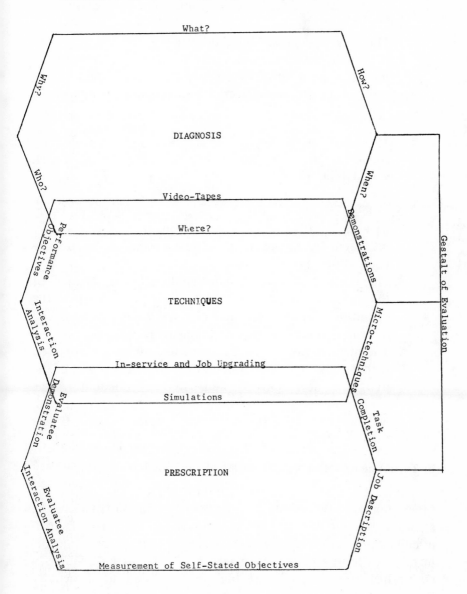

Figure 1-1

By Board or Superintendent Mandate

Advantages:

1. This is the quickest method of change.
2. It provides absolute conformity to the desired program of the ultimate authority, the board of education, and the chief administrative officer, the superintendent of schools.

Disadvantages:

1. The staff, with the voice in governance provided by collective bargaining laws, would probably not allow such a unilateral plan to take place without a great deal of upset.
2. Teacher and administrative tenure laws would probably have a negative effect on a plan that is unilaterally mandated by the board of education and/or the superintendent of schools.
3. There will be a lack of understanding among the staff of the reasons for the plan and the methodology of the operation unless a great deal of time is spent on advanced information prior to making the plan operational.
4. The major weakness of this mandated approach, however, is that those who are to be evaluated are not a part of the program development; and, in all probability, the announcement of the "wonderful new plan of evaluation" will be greeted by the staff with suspicion and with less than an enthusiastic response.

By Total Administration or Administrative Representatives

A representative group of administrators could include the superintendent, the assistant superintendent for instruction, the assistant superintendent for personnel services, the assistant superintendent for business affairs, the manager of transportation, the manager of food services, the manager of buildings and grounds, a senior high principal, a junior high principal and an elementary principal. Others, such as the curriculum director, the media director and the director of athletics could be added as desired. Even though all administrators, rather than a representative group, are included in the planning, this method has very similar advantages and disadvantages to that of the board and superintendent mandated program.

Advantages:

1. This is a rather rapid method of change.
2. It provides absolute conformity to the program desired by and designed by the consensus of the administrative staff.
3. It provides the positive advantage of involving all on-line supervisors as well as centralized administrators.

Disadvantages:

1. The staff, with the authority of collective bargaining laws to back up their demands, would probably not accept a plan of evaluation developed totally by administrative personnel.
2. Tenure laws would tend to negate the effectiveness of any evaluation plan developed by administration without significant staff involvement.
3. There will be a lack of understanding of the reasons for and details of the plan by members of the staff to be evaluated.
4. Because of a lack of meaningful staff involvement in the planning stages, suspicion, confusion and a lack of enthusiasm will be present within the staff if this methodology is utilized.

By Outside Experts or Outside Agencies

Advantages:

1. Outside experts and/or agencies, if carefully selected, will probably possess detailed information about the latest research findings and about a large number of operational plans.
2. The burden of total responsibility for any features of the evaluation plan that are not well received by the staff can be shifted to the outside expert and/or agency.
3. Hours of administrative and staff labor can be saved by employing an outside body to collect data, to formulate a plan and to present the proposal to all members of the school community.

Disadvantages:

1. Unless the employment conditions are carefully spelled out in advance, important internal policies will be determined by the outsiders who will not be responsible for the operation of the evaluation system.
2. A great deal of employee time will be spent in supplying background data to the outside experts.
3. This method could cost a considerable amount of money that could better be expended on some other aspect of the total school district program.
4. An evaluation plan developed by outsiders may very well not be accepted by the staff because of the methodology of development.

By Total Staff

Advantages:

1. This method allows maximum participation in the formulation of the total evaluative scheme.
2. This procedure permits total communication and it minimizes a lack of understanding and suspicion.

Disadvantages:

1. Thousands of man-hours could be wasted, relatively speaking, by this procedure. This would be especially true in a large school system.
2. If the study is to be completed on released time, this could be the most expensive plan of development that a school district could undertake.
3. This procedure will be the most inefficient of all possible methods. In fact, with the amount of staff turnover in most school districts, it may take so long to reach staff consensus that thirty percent of the total staff may be "new" from the time of initiation of the study.

By a Representative Sampling of All Staff Categories

The scheme of development that will have the greatest chance for success will be that which involves a representative group of teachers, administrators, custodians, secretaries, food service helpers, bus drivers, paraprofessionals and other employee groups. A group so selected could serve as a general steering committee; and sub-committees, with administrative representation and broad employee involvement, could work on the details to be developed within the general evaluative structure developed by the steering committee. It might well be meaningful to utilize outside experts, students and knowledgeable members of the lay community to assist the basic staff groups at the sub-committee levels.

Advantages:

1. Both the individuals to be evaluated and the individuals who are to conduct the evaluations are represented at all stages of planning.
2. Communication input and output is easily organized when such a broadly representative group plans the evaluative program.
3. Although it is not the most rapid method to use in planning an evaluative program, it is probably the most rapid method that can be used and still retain meaningful staff involvement.
4. The membership involved on committees can greatly assist in the selling and operational stages once the evaluative plan has been completed.
5. This method of involvement will probably best meet the desires of the staff members who are now guaranteed collective bargaining status for all conditions of work. However, it would be wise to develop the evaluation plan separate from any formalized collective negotiations procedure.

Disadvantages:

1. It will take more time, i.e., it will be less efficient than a mandated program.
2. It will be rather costly in terms of man-hours of effort expended.
3. The finalized evaluation scheme will not be acceptable to individuals and minority groups within the staff. Of course, this weakness is inherent to an even greater degree in the other plans which allow for less staff participation.

Other points that would be meaningful to consider when developing a procedural rationale are: (1) How will the committee membership be selected? (2) How may a total staff communication system be established during the programmatic developmental stage? (3) What shall be the duties and responsibilities of the steering committee and the sub-committee? (4) What types of informational inputs are necessary? (5) What completion time schedule seems appropriate? and (6) What are the budgetary and clerical needs of the committees?

SELECTING THE COMMITTEES:

In order that a committee becomes maximally functional, it is best to keep the committee's size from a minimum of ten members to a maximum of twenty-five members. This range will provide for broad representation and will still keep the total membership small enough to permit an ease of meaningful dialogue.

Although the committee members could be selected by the board of education, the superintendent of schools, or the administrative staff, the most favorable staff response will come if the committee membership is selected by employee group choice. A workable plan is to request each member of each employee group to nominate the three to five members that he feels would best represent him and the group on a staff evaluation steering committee. After the nominations are tallied those receiving consensus nominations should be asked to volunteer their service to the committee. Once a sufficient number of volunteers are identified, the steering committee will have a membership similar to the following: 6 teachers (2 from the elementary level, 2 from the junior high level and 2 from the senior high level), 3 custodians, 3 secretaries, 3 food service helpers, 3 paraprofessionals, 3 principals (1 from the elementary level, 1 from the junior high level and 1 from the senior high level) and 1 or more central office administrators.

This procedure also allows the peer groups to nominate those staff members who will best represent them; true leadership should thereby be located. Also, by allowing those individuals so nominated to volunteer their service, one retains the very important possibility of utilizing a committee that is highly motivated to undertake the task given it.

Similar representative sub-committees can be established for each employee group within the district. Each sub-committee should have representatives of each building or each grade level or some similar scheme. Each sub-committee should also have an on-line and a central office administrator as members. Each sub-committee chairman should be selected from the steering committee in order that immediate communication is built into and from the steering committee. Finally, depending upon the specific guide, sincere thought should be given to including students, appropriate lay persons within the school district and outside experts as members or as consultants to the sub-committee. For example, students might appropriately serve on the subcommittees for paraprofessionals and teachers, management specialists may well serve on the sub-committee for administrative evaluations and a resident who is in the construction trades might well serve on a committee dealing with the evaluation of maintenance personnel. Figure 1-2 presents the suggested committee structure and the communication flow diagram.

ESTABLISHING A COMMUNICATION SYSTEM:

The degree of acceptance of any finalized system of staff evaluation will be greatly dependent upon the quality and the quantity of communication provided during the process of evolution of the evaluation program. One aid to good positive communication is to select, within the nominated membership, those individuals who would represent the various school buildings within the district. Another prerequisite to positive communication is the scheduling of regularly spaced staff meetings at which the steering committee members and the sub-committee members can report the up-to-date developments, and at which the steering committee and sub-committee members can solicit comments, criticisms and suggestions from the total staff.

Although many other aids to positive communications could be added by the reader after he surveys his local situation, a final prerequisite to be remembered is the distribution of the written minutes of the steering committee and all sub-committees to each committee member, and each administrator. An updated set of minutes should also be placed on appropriate bulletin boards within each school building. Finalized decisions should also be duplicated and given to each employee within the group affected.

Membership Selection and Communication Flow Diagram

Steering Committee (volunteers, after nominations by total staff)

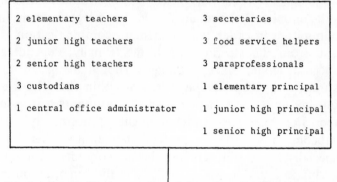

Sub-Committees (Chairmen selected from Steering Committee)

Teachers	Paraprofessionals	Secretaries	Others
10 Teachers	10 Paraprofessionals	10 Secretaries	10 Group Members
10 Students	10 Students	5 Lay Specialists	5 Lay Specialists
1 Administrator	1 Administrator	1 Administrator	1 Administrator
1 Consultant	1 Consultant	1 Consultant	1 Consultant

Communication Flow

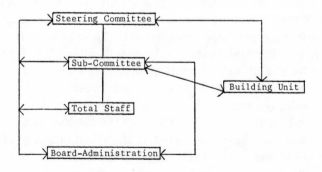

Figure 1-2

DEVELOPING THE DUTIES AND RESPONSIBILITIES:

The most effective way to cause a group working on a problem to stay within the framework of the problem and to work consistently towards its solution is to spell out the duties and responsibilities of the committee prior to commencing the problem solving process. The steering committee should develop its own duties and responsibilities, and it should develop the duties and responsibilities of each sub-committee in such a manner that the sub-committee's duties and responsibilities are consistent with those of the steering committee. Examples of statements of duties and responsibilities for a steering committee and for a sub-committee follow.

Duties and Responsibilities of the Steering Committee on Staff Evaluation

1. To review the current staff evaluation program to determine what is in existence; what degree of acceptance the program possesses by the employees, the administration and the board of education; and what, if anything, needs to be done to improve the current situation.
2. To study and review staff evaluation programs of superior quality which are operative in other schools, businesses and industries; and to determine whether or not elements of these programs should be built into the local evaluation scheme.
3. To review existing research in the area of staff evaluation and to utilize pertinent findings within the local program being developed.
4. To establish a philosophy to guide the development of a total, unified staff evaluation program.
5. To develop the pertinent objectives of the total district's staff evaluation program.
6. To provide the superintendent of schools and the board of education with an estimate of the human, material and monetary resources necessary to properly bring the total staff evaluation program to fruition.
7. To act as an advisory body to the superintendent of schools and the board of education. This responsibility

involves yearly progress reports and a final written statement on the staff evaluation plan which includes:

a. A statement of philosophy and objectives in the area of
   staff evaluation.
b. A complete description of the total program's mechanics, such as *who* evaluates, *what* is evaluated, *how* is
   evaluation to be done—including all necessary forms and
   descriptions, *when* shall evaluations take place, *where*
   shall evaluations be conducted and *why* is evaluation
   necessary.
c. A complete plan for publicity releases and in-service
   education and job upgrading..
d. A suggested time schedule within which the board of
   education and the superintendent of schools should
   establish the suggested staff evaluation program in an
   operational manner.
e. An estimate of the staff, materials, equipment, supplies
   and costs that are necessary to carry on the suggested
   program through implementation.
f. A listing of those elements which the committee members feel are imperative to program development or
   which are necessary to accomplish those items which are
   further requested by the superintendent of schools
   and/or the board of education.

**Duties and Responsibilities of the Sub-committee
on Custodial Staff Evaluation**

1. To review the current staff evaluation program as it applies
   to the custodial staff; and to determine what is in existence, what degree of acceptance the program possesses by
   the employees and the administration; and what, if anything, needs be done to improve the current situation.
2. To study and review custodial work standards, performance tasks and evaluation programs of superior quality
   which are operative in other schools, businesses and industries; and to determine whether or not elements of these
   programs should be incorporated into the local evaluation
   scheme.
3. To develop the objectives of the district's custodial staff

evaluation program (some elements will parallel other employee groups and others will be unique to the custodial unit).

4. To provide the steering committee with an estimate of the human, material and monetary resources necessary to properly complete the total program development.

5. To act as an advisory body to the steering committee on staff evaluation. This responsibility involves yearly progress reports and a final written summary of the total custodial staff evaluation plan.

6. To provide a suggested scheme for job upgrading and on-the-job training.

7. To provide a suggested time schedule within which the custodial staff evaluation program shall become operationally established.

8. To present an estimate of the staff, materials, supplies, equipment and costs necessary to carry out the suggested program of custodial evaluation.

9. To present a listing of those elements which the committee members feel are imperatives to program development or which are considered necessary to accomplish those things which are further requested by the steering committee.

TYPES OF INFORMATION INPUT:

Although each district's staff should develop the types of input informations that it deems necessary, basic informations that need be collected by every staff or group undertaking a program of staff evaluation are: (1) behavioral objectives—what needs be accomplished by the staff, stated in terms that will permit measurement of the results, (2) job descriptions—statements of specific tasks to be accomplished by each category of employee and by each employee within the district categories of the work force, (3) task standards—the square footage to be cleaned by the "average" custodial employee, the number of students to be served per hour by the "average" food service helper and many other such standards, (4) current and past systems and methods of staff evaluation utilized by the local district and, (5) staff evaluation programs, techniques and forms used by other school districts, businesses and industries.

TIME COMPLETION SCHEDULE:

Each district's staff will need determine a specific time completion schedule, and this schedule will vary in accordance with the stage of development of the existing staff evaluation program, available study time for committee members to do their work, the number of personnel to be involved in the planning of the staff evaluation program, available human and financial resources and numerous other local variables. A reasonable time completion schedule, however, would be:

Step I—6 months—collection of all desirable input informations.

Step II—6 months—development of a written statement of evaluation philosophy and objectives.

Step III—1 year—development of individual staff sub-committees' total evaluative schemes.

Step IV—6 months—development of a written total district's staff evaluation program.

Step V—6 months—implementation of a pilot feasibility study of the operational scheme that has been proposed.

Step VI—6 months—re-writing a modified total staff evaluation program based upon the findings of the pilot feasibility study.

Step VII—implementation of the total staff evaluation pro- as modified, district-wide.

Step VIII—periodic evaluation and modification of the total staff evaluation program over time as new variables are introduced into the local environment.

From the above time schedule, it is clear that a three-and-one-half year period is allowed for the development and implementation of the operational plan of staff evaluation. It is also clear that any program that is finalized, will need to be periodically monitored in order to allow the plan to remain current and relevant.

BUDGETARY AND CLERICAL NEEDS:

It is important that budgetary and clerical needs be clearly established and authorized *before* a group of staff members becomes involved in the time consuming and crucial task of developing and implementing a district-wide staff evaluation program. Specialized out-of-district consultants might be utilized. If so, the cost will be approximately $150 per day, plus expenses. Sufficient copies of desirable forms, informations and other materials from school districts, businesses and industries need be purchased. If there are a large number of sub-committees, a full-time secretary might be assigned to the project. If the school district is large, it might be wise to assign a full-time project manager to the staff evaluation project. Numerous other items need be determined and allowed for by those responsible for the development of the local staff evaluation program. For, if sufficient funds or assistance are not provided the committees, the total program is doomed to failure; and it will be most difficult to recreate a sufficient degree of interest in the future.

OUTLINING THE NECESSARY DECISIONS
TO BE MADE BY THE COMMITTEES

In formulating an overall system of staff evaluation decisions have to be made in six major decisional areas: (1) Why is evaluation needed or what are the purposes of evaluation? (2) What is to be evaluated or which forms of production or behavior are important to evaluate? (3) Who is to perform the evaluation? (4) When shall the evaluation take place or at what time of year, of day or at what duration of employment shall evaluation become important? (5) Where shall evaluation take place? and (6) How shall evaluation be conducted or which forms and procedures shall be utilized in performing the evaluative process?

Although greater depth of discussion shall be provided in subsequent chapters a brief resume of basic considerations shall serve to terminate this chapter:

WHY EVALUATE?

Evaluation might serve a single purpose or it might serve a multitude of purposes with varying techniques utilized in accordance with the purpose being served at the moment. The more comprehensive and basic reasons for conducting evaluations are: (1) to improve instruction, (2) to improve task performance, (3) to screen employees for future promotions and/or greater job responsibilities, (4) to differentiate staff assignments, (5) to grant merit or performance pay, (6) to provide a basis for tenure decisions or permanent appointments of civil service employees, (7) to let the individual employee know exactly what is expected of him and the degree to which his evaluator feels he is meeting his responsibilities, (8) to motivate employees to more closely attain their potential and to improve their job performance, (9) to provide information on the strengths and weaknesses of individual employees with the purpose of developing in-service and job upgrading programs to strengthen the individual in his areas of weakness and (10) to provide a variety of input information for the purpose of making wise administrative decisions in regard to the total staff, groups of employees and the individual employee.

WHAT IS TO BE EVALUATED?

Major decisions need be made as to the areas of performance to be evaluated and also as to the relative weighting that is to be given to each of the areas decided upon. Although many other areas can be added as the local needs determine, the three basic areas of personal characteristics, quantity of work produced and quality of work produced are crucial to any evaluative scheme. Quantitative factors will be more easily measurable for custodial personnel than teachers, while qualitative matters are easily determined in the number of errors made by typists. To arrive at a realistic listing of weighted factors for each personnel category is a major undertaking. However, such a weighted listing of factors must be done if a fair measurement system is to be determined.

WHO EVALUATES?

This question need be given considerable thought prior to the implementation of any total evaluation program. The answer may well be different for different school systems, and it could well be different for various evaluation purposes. Evaluation may be conducted by an individual or by a group.

The basic personnel that should be used in evaluation are the peers within the personnel work category, the individual worker's self evaluation and the immediate supervisor of the person being evaluated. Lay residents, students, central administrators and hired outside evaluators may be utilized if such use appears to be appropriate to the local evaluation plan that has been developed. Regardless of the ultimate number of personnel involved in the evaluation, there are two basic elements that must be included within each district's plan: (1) a self evaluation must be done by the employee and (2) the employee's immediate supervisor has to arrive at judgements based upon his evaluations when administrative decisions, such as whether or not to grant a teacher tenure, needs be made.

WHEN SHOULD EVALUATION BE CONDUCTED?

A complete system of evaluation will include pre-employment evaluation, a series of evaluations during employment and an exit interview to assist in improving evaluation. Decisions need be made as to how many evaluations are needed during the first year of employment, during subsequent years of employment. Also, decisions need be made as to which task performances are to be observed and how frequently they must be observed. Each of these decisions must be made prior to the planned evaluation program becoming operational.

WHERE SHALL EVALUATION TAKE PLACE?

Although this question is not as difficult as the *who, what, why, when,* and *how* queries, thought must be given to the various environmental conditions that are important to job performance. For example, a secretary may file and type in the office, but she might also record minutes of curriculum and/or negotiation sessions. Both of these duties are important and both performances need be considered in making an evaluation. Another example could well be an administrator who is hired to write and supervise state, Federal and foundation programs. He needs to be evaluated as to his performance with planning groups, in the offices of state and Federal officials and as to his performance in writing and implementing the programs within the local school district.

HOW SHALL EVALUATIONS BE CONDUCTED?

The *how* of evaluation will necessarily be different for each local district and it will differ with different groups and purposes over a period of time. Evaluation must be tied into performance objectives, and many different types of feedback must be provided the individual being evaluated. Also, one must resist the temptation of developing "one" evaluation program to fit all needs. Rather, one general program can contain identical elements, but a differentiated program must be developed to supplement the general program as different job categories and differing purposes are considered.

The major tools which will help to answer the *how* of evaluation are:

1. Developing criteria based upon student achievement and/or performance goals.
2. Developing criteria based upon work standards, such as square footage, numbers of persons serviced, number of words per minute and other standards.
3. Comparing the individual to employee models within his classification.
4. Comparing performance to job descriptions and statements of duties and responsibilities.
5. Recording performances by video and audio tape.
6. Comparing written behavioral objectives to the achievement level attained for the stated objectives.
7. Evaluating on-the-job interaction by the use of analytical tools.

Two

DETERMINING THE REASONS FOR
AND THE KEY FACTORS OF
A STAFF EVALUATION PROGRAM

Prior to the formulation of a plan of evaluation each district's staff must clearly identify the local reasons for evaluation. These reasons must be developed through meaningful dialogue, and the reasons decided upon need be continuously emphasized as new staff members enter the school district. The major reasons to be considered for inclusion or exclusion by all school districts are: (1) improvement of performance, (2) motivating employees to more closely attain their potential, (3) letting the employee know what is expected of him, (4) providing input information for administrative decisions, (5) determining whether or not tenure is to be granted, (6) determining merit pay provisions, (7) differentiating staff assignments, and (8) deciding on the staff characteristics to be developed in terms of educational, experiential and other factors important to local staff balance.

Before finalizing an evaluative scheme the important factors of the time periods during which evaluations are to be conducted; the methods to be utilized for determining job tasks and for determining classroom and other situational observations; and the individuals who are to serve as evaluators must be clearly delineated.

REASONS FOR EVALUATING

Staff evaluation that is well planned and clearly understood can be a tremendous asset in the positive upgrading of a total local school district's staff performance; an evaluation that is unilaterally decided upon, poorly planned, poorly communicated as to underlying rationale or not clearly understood by either the evaluatee or the evaluator can become one of the most destructive elements ever introduced into a local school district. The major reasons for a staff evaluation program will now be elaborated upon. Each of these reasons must be carefully discussed by a local district's staff prior to inclusion or exclusion within a local district's overall evaluation plan before the scheme becomes operational.

Improvement of Performance

The paramount reason for any program of evaluation must be the improvement of group and individual performance. Judgements as to whether or not performance has improved can be rather simple in the case of producing a quality controlled production unit, such as a lawn chair, in less time for a lower cost and a higher percentage of profit; or judgements can be rather complicated, such as a determination of the effect of an individual teacher or group of teachers on the increase in standardized test scores of a student or group of students. Many variables, such as the type of students, the instructional materials provided and the length of instruction time, must be controlled as much as possible in order to maximize objectivity.

Although evaluation in a school setting is a very complex task, it is possible and mandatory that educational institutions are held accountable for their levels of production. The staff of an educational institution is being held accountable by parents, taxpayers and other groups more than in any other time in history. It appears that a local school district's staff might better accept the responsibility and design its system of accountability. This is to be much preferred over a system of accountability that is designed and forced upon an educational institution by outside forces. It is also very true that a local school district's staff who wishes to improve group and individual performances can develop schemes to more closely delineate acceptable performance standards that can be measured and evaluated. For example, the typing teacher can certainly set speed, style and error margins for each individual student in his class, and he can set minimum class standards on a behavioral base that is measurable. A typing teacher could well set group behavioral standards that are measurable, such as: (1) 100% of the typing students will be able to type at a minimum speed of 35 words per minute with fewer than 3 errors on a 10 minute dictated exercise prior to the end of the class, (2) at least 75 percent of the students shall attain a speed of 45 words per minute with fewer than 3 errors on a 15 minute dictated exercise prior to the end of the class, and (3) a minimum of 60% of all the typing students shall pass the civil service typing exam prior to the end of the instructional term.

The typing teacher or the group of teachers assigned to typing instruction can thus be evaluated in terms of the achievement standards that have been agreed upon in advance of the course offering. This type of evaluation could also take into account other important matters such as the number of students who, on a free choice basis, choose one typing instructor over another; the typing staff can be partially evaluated on the job success of the graduates who pursue typing careers; and the cost of instruction can be compared, while holding the behavioral objectives constant, of one instructor with 25 students per class section, one instructor with a lay aid handling 150 students per class section, one instructor utilizing video tape or television lectures while the students are supervised by lay typists, or many other variations of the instructional mode.

The example of a typing teacher is rather clear; but many areas of industrial arts, drivers education, physical education and other areas are also rather easily subjected to performance evaluation. Certainly, many staff categories, such as cafeteria workers, secretarial employees, custodial employees and others, have numerous tasks which lend themselves to rather clear cut performance standards.

Attainment of Individual Potential

Student achievement, units of work produced per dollar

expended and other objective standards are crucial to a well planned evaluation program. However, no individual involved in developing or carrying out a plan of staff evaluation has the right to forget the affective domain and the human needs of each individual employee. A district that can display an impressive array of cost and production statistics that also has a disillusioned group of individual employees is a district that is headed towards major difficulties. A school district is not a human think tank or an automated production factory. It is, rather an assemblage of very human youths and adults who possess very real individualized needs.

Any evaluation plan must provide a scheme for the assessment of the individual employee's potential, a means of periodically assessing the degree of individual attainment, and a program for more closely attaining this stated potential over a period of time. Although the evaluator and the evaluatee need spend a great deal of time in detailing the staff members current performance level, the areas of improvement and the program that will lead to improvement, a few brief examples will serve to illustrate the point being made.

An elementary math teacher who is causing difficulties for her students at the next grade level because she has not developed the expertise to properly instruct her students in the methodologies or concepts of "new" math has a production potential that must be met. The solution could be as simple a one as taking a university course in "new" math structure, materials and teaching techniques; or the solution could well be to assign this teacher to a team teaching situation that would free him from responsibility for the teaching of mathematics. In any case, the students must be given the necessary type and quality of instruction, and the teacher must be made to feel comfortable, secure and capable of quality teaching.

A cleaner is not satisfactorily cleaning his assigned area which is equal to that assigned other cleaners who are performing in a satisfactory manner. The problem could well be that he has not been instructed in the proper use of the automated scrubbers; he is wasting time by hand-feeding the contents of individual waste baskets into the incinerator or a variety of other specific problems. The solution might be in-service education in the proper use of automated equipment, the assignment for a week to a cleaner who can demonstrate the proper scheduling of sub tasks or assigning a supervisor to the cleaner for the purpose of locating and solving the reasons for the individual's not attaining his potential.

A swimming coach is producing teams that are consistently beaten in competition with other schools with like enrollments, like numbers of student swimming candidates and students with the same swimming backgrounds prior to arriving as team members. In observation of the individual team member's performances it is determined that the individual's time improvements, and the time performances of the team as a whole, are not those that could be reasonably expected by checking the statistics on time performance for comparable groups of swimmers. On further investigation, it is discovered that the swimmers are slow off of the starting blocks, are not hitting their turns properly and lack the conditioning to remain competitive on the later laps of the races. The solutions might well be to send the swimming coach to clinics or to have him work with successful coaches on the techniques involved in getting off of the starting blocks and hitting the turns properly in order to cut time. Also, he should be provided assistance in the methodology of establishing stroke and endurance training programs for individual swimmers and in the means of recording and evaluating, over time, the individual swimmer's level of performance.

Informing the Employee of What is Expected

It is basic that an employee must know what is expected of him in order that he is able to attempt to perform in a satisfactory manner. It is unreasonable to criticize an employee for not performing his job in a satisfactory manner if he is not informed of his duties. Only as the expectancies are detailed, discussed and committed to writing can evaluation become possible.

Two prime means of letting an employee know what is expected are by the development of written job descriptions and by the establishment of priority performance objectives. Job descriptions should be developed by the supervisor listing what he expects to be accomplished, the employee listing exactly what tasks he is currently performing, and agreement being reached and committed to writing on the finalized listing of job responsibilities

and the sub tasks to be performed. A listing of priority performance objectives over a period of time, such as one year, also
assists the employee in knowing what is expected of him. Such
priority objectives need be developed through dialogue between
the evaluator and the evaluatee in order to be of maximum
effectiveness.

For example, a building principal may have 50 tasks in his
job description, but one priority performance objective for the
current year might well be to establish a workable system of
teacher aides and volunteer parents that will permit the teaching
staff to spend a much greater percentage of their time on the
teaching act. Another example might be that of a secretary who is
wasting a great deal of valuable time because her dictation skills
have diminished. The secretary and her immediate supervisor may
well agree that a priority performance objective for the next
six-month-period would be to raise this skill performance by a
specifically stipulated amount or degree.

Providing Input Informations for Administrative Decisions

One positive by-product of a sound evaluative program is the
production, recording and storage of masses of informations that
can be drawn upon at future times for the purpose of making
knowledgeable administrative decisions. It would be difficult to
list all the possible administrative decisions that might be based
upon the informations collected during the operation of a comprehensive evaluative program. Each district's staff needs to determine what part, and to what degree, staff evaluations are to play
in those administrative decisions that are deemed important to the
school district's welfare.

A few examples of usage, however, will serve a demonstrative
purpose at this juncture. Evaluative informations might well be
used in the development of a teacher team. Such informations
could be utilized in determining staff promotions; in assigning
categories of staff in such a way that the tasks performed are
assigned to the lowest salaried staff category that is capable of
acceptably performing the tasks; and in assigning staff members to
tasks on such variables as age, sex, degree of health, personality
characteristics and other variables when such factors are important
to the specific assignment.

Tenure Determinations

In practically every school system there are legal responsibilities which necessitate an administrative or board of education decision to be made in regards to the tenure status of employees. In many states a decision must be made and recorded at the end of the second year, fifth year or other time period of employment. Normally, once tenure is granted an employee it becomes extremely difficult to eliminate an unwanted staff member. At the very least, the burden of proof and the limited reasons that are legally available for dismissal make the granting of tenure a very crucial decision point to be considered when comprising the total evaluative scheme.

The board of education, administration and other staff members of a school district should openly face this issue, and a determination should be made as to how this particular decision is to be fitted into the overall plan of evaluation. If proper emphasis is placed upon the careful screening of candidates prior to initial employment, upon the task of improving job performance of all employees, upon the basic goal of providing assistance to the individual in overcoming his weaknesses; the number of employees who are not granted tenure will comprise a very small percentage of the total staff. In any case, this important decision should be made on the basis of clear cut documentation which is known throughout his employment by the employee.

Determining Merit Pay

The issue of merit pay can become very controversial, and a great deal of staff involvement needs be had if this feature is to be incorporated into the total scheme of evaluation. Such matters as limits on the percent of staff to receive such pay incentives, the length of time the employee needs be employed before he qualifies for merit pay, the standards upon which merit pay is to be granted and numerous other problems need be openly resolved prior to building this feature into the evaluation program. It is important to remember that a tentative plan could be initiated for a trial period prior to making a final decision. This pilot program could well allow a creative feature to be ultimately incorporated, whereas it may well be eliminated if a premature prior decision is made.

A creative planning group would do well to look at various means of providing rewards for the high production employee. For example, if all cleaners are assigned the same number of rooms or the same square footage to be cleaned up to agreed upon standards, the number of hours spent on cleaning may be a variable well worth looking at in a close matter. If Cleaner X completes his assigned areas in an acceptable manner in six hours, he could be allowed to go home two hours early. Surely if one were to compute an hourly wage, Cleaner X has received merit pay.

In any case, it behooves any group who is held responsible for the development of a comprehensive staff evaluation plan to look closely at the fact that all employees do not perform at the same level. Whether or not this is to be recognized by monitary or other means is really the key question to be considered.

Differentiating Staff Assignments

Differing assignments call for differing knowledges, skills and personality characteristics. This is an indisputable fact. Whether one assumes that all teachers, or any other employee groups, are equally qualified to perform their assignments by reason of degree, number of years of experience or some other variables that may or may not be pertinent; or whether one assumes that the assessment of knowledges, skills and personality characteristics are important when making specific staff assignments becomes a crucial matter to be discussed by any group who is devising an evaluative scheme.

It probably is important that a maintenance employee have excellent health, a librarian doesn't look like a bookworm who will turn students off, a physical education teacher is not so obese that, by example, the girls and boys are negatively effected, a member of a team teaching group is able to get along well with other people, an advanced biology or math teacher has training and/or experience beyond that needed by a teacher of elementary biology, an instrumental music teacher is also a capable performer in his own right, and numerous other examples that could be cited. These variables must be assessed as part of a comprehensive evaluation program.

The math teacher who does not have advanced training might well be an excellent instructor of general math, but he might be a disaster in calculus. The obese female physical education teacher might turn off senior high girls, but she may do an excellent job and be well accepted by elementary youngsters. The team teacher who has problems getting along with others on a total impact team might do very well when assigned to a self contained classroom. The instructor who has problems with large group lectures might be an excellent television instructor, or he might do very well with small group instruction.

The assessment of these variables are imperative to an excellent program of staff evaluation. The collected data based on these variables will go a long way towards meeting the dual purposes of providing the students with the best instruction possible and towards utilizing the human resources of the district in such a manner that the staff is content and productive.

Development of Important Staff Characteristics

An evaluative scheme should allow the development, through on-the-job training and in-service experiences, of those important staff characteristics that provide the desirable staff balance. Assessment by means of evaluation will allow the factual basis to be formulated to permit the total staff blend desired.

If the concept of the school district is to place the classroom teacher in the role of coordinator of his staff of teacher aides, teacher coordinators in specialized subjects, determiner of pretaped programmed materials and other important role variations, it is important that the ability to perform in this manner is assessed through evaluation. This role is much different than the one expected of a self-contained classroom teacher who is assumed to be all things to each pupil in his charge.

Multi-media usage, team teaching, television instruction, programmed learning, computerized instruction, modular time block scheduling, diagnostic-prescriptive staff teams, small group and large group instruction, learning resource teachers, independent study, work-study approaches, and many other concepts call for teaching roles that cannot be standardized. Other employee groups also call for the development of various staff characteristics. For example, the baker, the cook, the cashier, the inventory clerk, the food service helper and the on-line server all work within the cafeteria operation, but the characteristics needed many times greatly vary.

Any evaluative program needs to determine the characteristics needed to successfully carry out a specific assignment, assess the characteristics that are present in each employee, provide assistance in developing the needed characteristics if they are nonexistent, and make staff assignments in accordance with the knowledge so collected. It is imperative that the comprehensive evaluation program have a plan for the development of desirable characteristics when such characteristics are not possessed by an individual staff member or by a group of staff members.

WHEN AND WHERE SHOULD EVALUATIONS BE CONDUCTED?

When evaluations are to be conducted is a question that needs be resolved by any group planning a total program of evaluation prior to operationalizing the plan. How many evaluations per year? Does a successful long term employee need as many evaluations? How much employee time can and should be freed to conduct evaluations? What should be the length of the evaluation, and should there be varying lengths for varying evaluative purposes? How frequently should evaluations be conducted for a long-term successful employee who is performing at a lower level than in previous years? How frequent should be the evaluations when a new instructional technique is introduced to experienced staff members? Other related questions also become areas of concern when answering the major question of when should evaluations be conducted.

A reasonable proposal, considering the answers to the questions asked in the previous paragraph, would be a minimum of one evaluation by students (for teachers only) each year, three evaluations per year by each employee's immediate supervisor and three evaluations per year by at least one of the employee's fellow workers. This could be reduced to two per year by the supervisor and fellow workers in the case of tenured employees, and the numbers could be increased as deemed necessary for those employees who are performing at a questionable level. The evaluations should be reasonably spaced throughout the year.

The length of each evaluation should be one hour, with flexibility built in on a need basis. Video tapes of specific performances could be utilized over various time periods, and the review and evaluation by the employee and the evaluator could be conducted in an informal atmosphere for any length of time desired.

A reasonable compromise for the three evaluations to be conducted by the supervisor and the peer might be to have one evaluative visit when requested by the employee, one which is requested in advance by the evaluator and one at which the evaluator visits unannounced. These three situations should provide a good random sampling of the employee's work.

The job tasks to be evaluated and the observational environment for the evaluative visits should be determined in advance. In the case of an elementary teacher one visit may be requested for the purpose of observing reading instruction. A personnel director may be visited during employee interviews. A speech therapist may be visited while working with three separate students. A groundsman may be visited while dressing the baseball field. The observational environment should also be predetermined. A member of a teaching team may need be observed while instructing a group of students in his classroom, while working with an individual student on a learning disability and while planning the next week's instructional program with other teaching team members. Whatever decisions are made in terms of tasks to be evaluated and the environment in which the evaluation is to take place, these should not be matters left to chance.

WHO SHOULD EVALUATE?

The final decisions to be made as to which persons need conduct evaluations must be made after much dialogue among members of the group planning the comprehensive plan of staff evaluation. The types of evaluators that need be discussed are: (1) peers within the employee's group, (2) students (in the case of teaching staff), (3) self evaluations, (4) lay residents, (5) outside paid consultants, (6) central office administrators, and (7) immediate supervisors. The arguments for and against the inclusion of each type of evaluator will be presented. It should be stressed, however, that these are not either/or decisions, and it might be best to utilize a combination of the evaluator types in a local district's situation.

Peer Evaluation

The evaluation by one's peers seems a very logical method of achieving an evaluation. However, there are advantages and disadvantages to using one's peers as evaluators.

The advantages of peer evaluations are:

1. A fellow worker assigned the same task possesses more in-depth knowledge of the requirements of the specific assignment than any other individual. Who might better judge a reading specialist than another reading specialist? Who might better judge a cleaner than another cleaner assigned the same tasks within a comparable square footage area?

2. A fellow worker is best equipped to provide an objective analysis of strengths and weaknesses, and he is also best able to provide detailed assistance in overcoming the weaknesses that have been located.

3. A comradarie exists between co-workers that makes the evaluation process less threatening, and this fact puts the person being evaluated more at ease.

4. A peer evaluation system produces better morale throughout the entire employee group because peers are placed in a helpful relationship.

The disadvantages of peer evaluations are:

1. The peer evaluator may by myopic in vision; and. therefore, he may not understand the total district's needs. This could cause some very important information to be completely missed.

2. The peer evaluator is placed in the unfair position of evaluator when he has no authority or responsibility to make judgements about the quantity and quality of a fellow worker's production level. This responsibility is an administrator's responsibility, and the administrator should shoulder this complete load. The answer to this quandry might be different, dependent upon the purposes of the peer evaluations and the uses which are to be made of the evaluation data.

3. The peer evaluator will not be objective in his evaluation since he is a member of the same employee group. The tendency to whitewash all employees may be increased with the presence of unions and collective bargaining.

4. The peer evaluation may conflict with that of the immediate administrative supervisor who has to make recom-

mendations as to hiring, firing and promotion. Peer positive evaluations may undergird his case and hinder the
administrator's decision. At the very least, the administrator might have to spend many hours with union stewards in
defending his decision if the administrator presents a
negative overall evaluation of an employee.

5. A peer evaluation could lead to resentment of a co-worker
by the evaluatee if the evaluation is not favorable. This, in
turn, could lead to intra-group conflict which would be
detrimental to the total school district's operation.

6. Peer evaluations could be very costly when the amount of
released time from the prime duties of the evaluators is
computed.

Student Evaluation

On the surface it appears logical to involve the recipients of
the educational enterprise in the evaluation of the teachers who
are hired to oversee the instructional program at the student level.
There are, however, advantages and disadvantages to the involvement of students in the process of teacher evaluation. Tradi-
tionally, it is assumed that the disadvantages of student evaluations will increase as the age of the students performing the
evaluations decrease. Certainly, it would be wise to at least
attempt student evaluation at the senior high level, and if this
proves successful, attempt student evaluation at lower age levels.

Advantages of student evaluations:

1. The user (student) is best able to evaluate the giver
(teacher).

2. Students are in daily contact with a number of teachers;
and therefore, have the best basis upon which to make a
comparative judgement of teacher production.

3. The number of evaluators is greatly increased and the
evaluation becomes much broader in scope. Also, the
biased evaluations can quickly be discarded, and a large
number of evaluations will remain.

4. This method would not add any dollar cost to the process.

Disadvantages of student evaluations:

1. Students may tend to provide low evaluations for the strict
teacher, the teacher who gives a great deal of work, the

teacher who is a low marker or the teacher of a subject
that is mandatory and considered boring by the majority
of students.

2. Students are too immature to evaluate teacher performance.

3. A student may influence other students to rate a teacher
poorly because he has a particular axe to grind with the
teacher being evaluated. Youngsters sometimes have
cliques and a single student's dislike for a teacher might
cause an overall negative bias to be present in the evaluations.

The writer does not personally subscribe to the thoughts
presented in the disadvantages listed. Should the local district's
evaluation committee have such concerns, student evaluations
could be tried on a pilot basis and a final decision made on the
basis of the results. In fact, a pilot feasibility study is always a
good approach when doubt exists as to the inclusion of any
category of evaluator within the overall evaluative scheme.

Self Evaluation

The main advantage of a self evaluation is that the employee
knows best his goals; and, therefore, he should best be able to
judge the degree to which he is able to achieve his goals. The main
disadvantage of a self evaluation is that some individuals con-
stantly overrate or underrate their performance.

Self evaluations coupled with other types of evaluations can
be most meaningful in a comprehensive evaluative scheme. The
writer has developed and used the form shown in Figure 2-1 with
numerous school principals. The self evaluation is completed by
the principal prior to his conference with the superintendent. The
superintendent has also completed a similar evaluative instrument
prior to the conference. These instruments, coupled with job
descriptions and agreed upon yearly performance objectives, have
proven to be very useful tools in the evaluation of building
principals

Principals React to This: I have heard principals state, "It is
good to change a teacher's grade level after a few years." Is this
also a positive recommendation at the principalship level?

Administrative Evaluation Guide Sheet

Directions: Read and react to the following questions. These will
serve as the basis for the evaluative discussion between
yourself and the superintendent. This will be a two-way
evaluation.

1. Professional Growth - What have you done in the past year?

2. What local school related programs and activities have you
participated in, and how did this benefit you and the District?

3. I possess an (excellent, average, or poor) working relationship
in the following: Why?

    a. Non-professional Staff

    b. Teachers

    c. Students

    d. Other Administrators - Building, Central Office

    e. Lay people

    f. Board of Education

4. I possess the following personal characteristics to a (high,
average, or low) degree:

    a. Dependability

    b. Initiative

    c. Creativity

    d. Give and take suggestions

    e. Self-confidence

    f. Ethical behavior

5. I have (improved, stayed the same, decreased) communications -
name the specific ways with:

    a. Non-professional Staff

    b. Teachers

    c. Students

    d. Other Administrators - Building, Central Office

Figure 2-1

    e. Lay people

    f. Board of Education

6. In the area of Instruction I have:

    a. Visited classrooms - For what purposes?

                          - What did I gain?

                          - How did my visits help teachers and kids?

    b. I have studied the following instructional innovations this

        year _____.

    c. I have made education better this year by doing the following

        things with my staff meetings _____.

    d. I feel I have made the following contributions to a K-12,

        district-wide approach this year _____.

7. In the area of management I have:

    a. Carried out an assigned task by my superior in such a manner

        that he did not have to prod me to finish, nor did he have to

        check my work for accuracy.

    b. I have made the following "hard" decisions in the past year

        _____

    c. I have modified my role because of negotiations in the follow-

        ing ways (positive and/or negative) _____

    d. I have played the following roles (explain) in terms of:

        (1) Board policy

        (2) Budget campaign

        (3) Annexation campaign

        (4) Budgetary control

8. If I had complete authority, I would make the following changes

    for next year in the area of:

    a. Physical plant

Figure 2-1 (cont.)

    b. Custodial service

    c. Purchasing

    d. Secretarial service

    e. Hot lunch

    f. Specialized teachers (including County)

    g. Playground arrangement and usage.

    h. My administrative decision making authority and responsibility.

    i. Any others

9. I feel that the following things that I have done this year could have been done as well by a lay person _____

10. I feel that the following things that I have done could not have been done as well by a lay person _____

SUMMARY AND CONCLUSIONS

11. I feel that my greatest contribution in the past year has been ____
    _____.

12. I feel my greatest area of weakness in the past year has been ____
    _____.

13. I intend to do the following things to improve myself next year _
    _____.

14. I feel that I can contribute the following to the administrative team next year _____.

15. My hopes for improving my building's and/or the District's instructional situation next year are _____.

Superintendent's summary of specifics:

    a. Strengths (incidents)

    b. Weaknesses (incidents)

    c. Recommendations _____

Lay Resident's Evaluation

The inclusion of lay residents as part of an evaluation team may well be the most controversial of all proposals to be discussed. There are rather obvious advantages and disadvantages to the inclusion of this category of evaluator.

Advantages:

1. Residents pay the bills for a local school district's operation, and they have an inherent right to evaluate the production level.
2. A staff is daily dealing with the sons and daughters of lay residents, and the staff should be held accountable for their production by the parents of the student recipients.
3. Residents provide a no cost method of broadening the base of evaluation.
4. Residents, if carefully selected, possess a great deal of expertise in specific areas. For example, an auto mechanic should be well-qualified to evaluate a teacher of auto mechanics; an executive secretary should provide an objective evaluation of a teacher of secretarial practice, a custodial supervisor at an industrial plant should be able to constructively evaluate a school district's custodial staff, and so forth.

Disadvantages:

1. It would be harmful to permit parents to evaluate teachers who have the parent's child in class. This could lead to many conflicts.
2. It would be very difficult to choose among those parents who volunteer to serve as evaluators, and many residents who are not qualified to evaluate may volunteer.
3. A resident with a negative mind set towards the school may insist on being an evaluator as a means of showing the institution the correct method of conducting its business.
4. Residents would not volunteer to be put on the spot as evaluators.

It should be noted that the inclusion of residents as evaluators can broaden the dimensions of the evaluation. A district may wish to involve them in planning the scheme of evaluation if not in the actuality of the evaluative process. If residents are included as evaluators they should be selected on the basis of serving very specific purposes. Not to include residents as evaluators would deny that much expertise exists in the local educational community.

Outside Paid Consultants

The major advantages of involving outside paid consultants as evaluators are: (1) They can provide a degree of expertise that is normally not possessed by the local district's staff, (2) They possess knowledge of the most current research findings and the most current successful evaluative schemes, and (3) They are unbiased in their evaluations because they have nothing personally at stake at the local district level. The major disadvantages of involving outside paid consultants as evaluators are: (1) The cost to the district could be prohibitive, and (2) They may well evaluate the staff in terms of their value systems, and neglect to evaluate the staff on those items that are considered to be of major importance by the local district's clientele.

Central Office Administrators

The major advantages of involving central office administrators are: (1) They provide a double check against the evaluation of the employee's immediate supervisor, (2) They are normally the final decision makers for hiring, firing, promotions and granting tenure; and, therefore, they must become evaluators, (3) They are highly specialized in areas such as curriculum development, business, personnel and other areas; and they bring great in-depth expertise to the evaluation process, and (4) They usually have ultimate accountability for the operation of the entire school district; and, thus, they must assess the level of production of the various employee groups. The major disadvantages of including central office administrators in the evaluative process are: (1) They are too far removed from the classroom, the cleaning station and so forth to be able to objectively evaluate an individual employee, (2) They are paid large salaries and have major coordination responsibilities. Therefore, to utilize them as evaluators, constitutes a relative waste of human resources, and (3) They could cause resentment by and moral problems for the immediate administrative supervisor by arriving at evaluations which conflict with those of the immediate supervisor.

If the local group does not decide to utilize central office administrators on a regularized basis as evaluators, they may wish to build in a system of evaluative appeals that would make use of central office talent. In any case, the overall plan of evaluation must be agreed to by the central office administrators as they shoulder the ultimate burden of public accountability for the production level of the local school district's staff.

Immediate Supervisors

Each district must include the staff's immediate supervisor in any evaluative scheme. The immediate supervisor is directly responsible for the day-by-day production level of every employee assigned to his charge. The inclusion of the immediate supervisor is not a matter for debate. The role that the immediate administrative supervisor is to play in the total evaluative scheme, however, is very much the business of the group that is assigned the responsibility for a total district's evaluation program.

Advantages of supervisory evaluations:
1. His training and job assignment makes him the best qualified person to conduct the evaluations.
2. He has day-by-day responsibility, and he must evaluate if he is to be held accountable.
3. He has the greatest number of day-to-day contacts with all staff members assigned to his building, and he should be best able to provide valid, unbiased comparative staff evaluations, and
4. His evaluations will have more impact on the building's staff than that of any other single evaluator.

Disadvantages of supervisory evaluations:

1. The principal's and/or supervisor's image interferes with the objectivity of the evaluative process.
2. The principal and/or immediate supervisor many times has not taught in a classroom, cleaned floors, baked food and so forth for years. Therefore, he is not capable of producing an objective evaluation based upon current knowledge or methodology.

3. The supervisor does not know what good production levels are for such a large variety of tasks. Can one building principal really be expected to be knowledgeable and objective in the evaluation of art, music, physical education, graphics, exceptional education, media, English and so forth?

4. The supervisor many times will be reluctant to "call them as he sees them" for fear of staff morale problems, for concern about his own acceptance by the staff, or for a variety of similar reasons.

5. The supervisory salary is normally higher than that of many other categories of employees. He also has broad based coordination assignments. His use as an evaluator would be wasteful of money and of human resources.

It is well to terminate this discussion by suggesting that the group charged with the responsibility of planning a total district's evaluation scheme utilize an eclectic approach. The involvement of various types of evaluators for a variety of specific purposes will provide a more positive overall scheme than settling on a single type of evaluator for the total evaluative process.

Three

IDENTIFYING AREAS TO BE
EVALUATED AND TECHNIQUES
TO BE UTILIZED

Once the local district's decision makers have decided that they wish to develop a total staff evaluation program, once they have decided on a comprehensive rationale to guide the total composition of the evaluative program, once they have determined the reasons for conducting evaluations, and once they have decided upon who is to perform the evaluations; the difficult tasks of deciding which criteria to utilize and which techniques to be used in accomplishing the total evaluative program remains.

This chapter will present a discussion of the techniques of PERT (Program Evaluation and Review Technique), Cost Benefit Analysis, Cost Effectiveness Analysis, simulation experiences, video and audio recordings, and interaction analysis techniques. The importance of the techniques of rating scales, of performance measurement compared to stated behavioral objectives, and of performance measurement compared to statements of job descriptions will also be mentioned. The chapter will terminate by presenting the development of criteria based upon student achievement, upon stated performance goals, and upon comparisons of individuals' performances to those of employee models.

PERT AND CPM

Both of these techniques were originally developed for governmental purposes. The missile industry utilized these techniques to a large extent throughout its space development program. Both techniques provide for the detailing of every event to be performed in sequence over the allotted time for the total project's development. In basic function, the techniques of PERT and CPM pinpoint the tasks that need be performed before the next task can be undertaken. The minimum and maximum time allotted for each sub-task is determined, and any operational deviation from the established time and task chart is readily identified by a periodic review of the performance to date.

Although there are some technical differences between the PERT and CPM systems, the reader has many materials available explaining the details of both systems. One comprehensive volume on the topics is that written by Archibald and Villoria.[1] For the purposes of this volume a general example will be presented that would allow for either a PERT or a CPM application.

A very simplified partial example which does not utilize the specific terminology of PERT or CPM would be the repair and painting of a six room wing of a school building by the district's maintenance staff (although specific times are not listed, the events are listed in a time sequence):

Step #1—Evaluation of the needed maintenance by the supervisor of maintenance, the plumber, the electrician, the carpenter and the painting supervisor.

Step #2—Estimation of the budget, the work force needed and the length of time and number of each category of worker needed, the equipment necessary and the supplies and materials on hand and to be ordered to complete the assignment.

Step #3—Ordering of all supplies, equipment and materials needed to complete the assignment. Obviously, hard to obtain items must be ordered well in advance in order to assure delivery on the site at the time needed. Plumbing

---

[1] Archibald, Russell D. and Villoria, Richard L., Network-Based Management Systems (PERT/CPM). New York: John Wiley and Sons, Inc., 1967.

and electrical supplies will be needed prior to carpentry supplies, and carpentry supplies need be on the job prior to painting supplies.

Step #4—Scheduling of the work force. Perhaps two plumbers and one electrician could be scheduled for a thirteen day period, and they could work simultaneously. Four carpenters could then, perhaps, be scheduled for a one week period, and it might be cheaper to employ them for a sixth day at overtime pay in order to facilitate the job. Finally, six painters could be utilized for a one week period, and one painter could be utilized for an additional three days to complete the finish work.

This oversimplified example would permit evaluation to take place by evaluating the progress of each work unit when compared to the PERT or CPM chart. Evaluation would also be possible by inspecting the quality and quantity of work produced by one painter compared to another and other such comparisons.

Advantages:

1. Both PERT and CPM cause planners to detail all sub-tasks involved in completion of a total project.
2. Both techniques cause planners to sequence all sub-tasks in such a manner that one element, such as man power variations or delivery dates of necessary materials, is thought through to completion in such a manner that total project efficiency is protected.
3. Both techniques permit the immediate identification of trouble spots, and they allow a look at any adjustments that need to be made in the entire project instead of dealing with such problems in isolation.
4. Both techniques allow the pinpointing of detailed responsibility, and this permits all other elements of the total project to focus directly upon the individual who has the responsibility for the problem.

Disadvantages:

1. Both CPM and PERT are complex techniques and will not pay dividends if applied to small projects.
2. Both techniques originated in areas other than education

and very few educational applications have been made to date.

3. Although these techniques hold great potential for the future in the area of education, the local district must be staffed with creative individuals who also have studied the techniques.

COST-BENEFIT AND COST-EFFECTIVENESS ANALYSIS

Cost-Benefit Analysis is a technique which involves the definition of objectives that can be measured, and the determining of solutions to obtaining the objectives that can be quantified in terms of the cost of the alternate solutions. Of course, considering all constraints, the least expensive method of obtaining the results should be accepted. This technique could be involved in such decisions as whether or not to buy dictation equipment for selected secretaries, whether or not to buy scrubber-polishers for the cleaning personnel, whether or not to buy high intensity ovens for the cooks and bakers and other similar decisions. This technique also can be utilized in decisions as to whether to strip wax the school floors weekly, monthly, quarterly or yearly. It could also be utilized when determining whether or not a cost benefit would accrue by installing carpet rather than tile and whether it would be a cost benefit to purchase equipment rather than add additional grounds staff and many other similar decisions. The implications for employee evaluations are clear: a custodian in a carpeted school must be evaluated on work standards that are different than a custodian in a tiled school with a great deal of mechanical equipment or one assigned a tiled school with only hand equipment. A final example would be a decision as to whether or not to hire teacher aides. If aides were hired this would change the duties, and thus the evaluations, of the teacher performance in certain areas.

Cost-Effectiveness Analysis is a technique very similar to that of Cost-Benefit Analysis. The major difference is that this term is applied to qualitative decisions which do not permit themselves to be easily quantified in terms of dollars and cents.

Advantages:

1. These techniques utilize stated objectives, and this process

permits evaluation of the costs and the efficiencies of tasks performed by various categories of staff.

2. These techniques force differentiated staff assignments in such a manner that each task can be assigned to the staff category which is most capable of performance at the lowest cost.

3. These techniques assist staff evaluation in that a clear-cut delineation of labor is achieved.

4. These techniques assist staff evaluation in that they help order the tasks to be performed in such a manner that only those tasks that are of major importance to the job assignment will be evaluated. For example, a teacher will not receive a negative evaluation on maintenance of attendance registers, collecting milk monies, supervising lunch rooms and so forth.

Disadvantages:

1. It may take a great deal of time to collect the amount of relevant input data necessary to make cost-benefit and cost-effectiveness decisions.

2. A large expenditure of funds may be necessary for in-service programs that will teach employees to write objectives in behavioralistic terms.

3. Much time may need be spent in convincing the staff that this "new" approach will assist them in doing a better job of achieving goals.

SIMULATION TECHNIQUES

Simulation techniques provide means of duplicating actual tasks prior to the assumption of real job responsibility. A simulation may be as simple as pre-dictated letters to be put in actual business form by a new secretary, or a simulation may be as complicated as a series of micro-teaching experiences which are consistently evaluated by the employee and the evaluator immediately after each ten minute teaching performance. In such situations the desired behavior is clearly defined prior to the teaching act, and the evaluation zeros in on a very specific and measurable behavior. Simulations assist in in-service training, and they can be put to use as a daily means of correcting observable staff weaknesses.

Advantages:

1. Simulations provide real life work tasks without running the risks of on-the-job failures.
2. Simulations can provide immediate evaluation and reinforcement to the employee being evaluated.
3. Simulations can save a great deal of time in job training, and they can provide an environment which eliminates the uncontrolled variables existent in a real life situation.

Disadvantages:

1. Simulation is not real life, and many unplanned incidents intervene in real life working environments.
2. Simulation requires that a great deal of time be spent in contriving realistic exercises and experiences.

VIDEO AND AUDIO RECORDINGS

Recordings are useful tools to use in any evaluation scheme. Like all evaluative techniques recordings have advantages and disadvantages.

Advantages:

1. Recordings can be made of practically any job task performed regardless of the category of personnel to be evaluated.
2. Recordings can be stored for use at any time in the future. They can be reviewed by the evaluator and/or the evaluatee alone or together. They can also be reviewed many times for multiple purposes.
3. Multiple recordings over a time period can record progress towards the achievement of an objective.
4. Recordings can be erased and reused. They, therefore, provide a relatively inexpensive means of collecting data for evaluative purposes.

Disadvantages:

1. Many employees do not react in a normal manner when a video tape camera or an audio recorder is used.
2. Some time must be spent in training employees, other than

the individual's being evaluated, to operate video tape equipment in the proper manner.

3. Numerous costs may be involved for tape recorders and video cameras. It may also cost a good deal of money for tapes if they are to be stored and not reused over a lengthy period of time. These costs might become prohibitive.

INTERACTION ANALYSIS TECHNIQUES

In the 1960's the attempts at teacher evaluation seemed to switch from data collection by means of ratings to data collection of behavioral observations on a variety of objective instruments. The various schemes use check lists, matrix analysis and other formats. In most cases these schemes call for trained observers. Rather than discussing any of the specific plans at this juncture, the reader is referred to an anthology that is edited by Simon and Boyer.[2]

Advantages:

1. These methods represent the most recent method of investigation into classroom evaluation.
2. These methods observe pupil and teacher behaviors on a very systematic basis, and many of these methods allow for the collections of large masses of data over relatively short periods of time.
3. These methods provide teachers with observational feedback data about the discrepancies between their intents and their performances.

Disadvantages:

1. Monies and staff time has to be allotted for a training program for those individuals who are to serve as observers.
2. The validity of these instruments would be in jeopardy with some change of observers.
3. Sole reliance on these observational techniques may not allow a comprehensive evaluation program to be applied to

---

[2]Simon, Anita and Boyer, E. Gil, *Mirrors for Behavior.* Philadelphia, Penn.: Research for Better Schools, Inc., January, 1968.

all staff categories. At this point this research is directed towards classroom teachers.

These relatively new tools hold much promise for the future of teacher evaluation and teacher improvement systems. Any local group planning a total district's evaluative program should give very serious consideration to inclusion of these techniques into the ultimate program developed.

RATINGS SCALES

Although questionnaires, inventories and anecdotal records are sometimes used for teacher evaluations, a large number of districts rely on rating scales. Rating scales usually compare the teacher being evaluated with other teachers, established norms or with some other standard that has been devised and agreed upon. These scales may have a series of descriptive terms, a continuum that can be used as a comparative graph, or a weighted numerical system. Rating scales must be weighted in order to provide a true measure of those items and/or characteristics which are of a higher order of priority. Without a weighting system rating scales are of very little value.

Advantages:

1. Rating scales are normally rather simple to complete.
2. Identical forms may be used by different evaluators and stored for comparative purposes.
3. Item analysis can be conducted on rating scales, and strengths and weaknesses of categories of personnel can be identified.
4. Weightings of sub-scale items can be determined in order that the higher priority of behaviors and/or characteristics can be given greater importance by any evaluator who utilizes the scale.

Disadvantages:

1. Rating scales normally are not written in behavioral terms which are free from interpretive bias by various users.
2. Rating scales that are not weighted leave the evaluator with the assumption that all rating sub-items are of equal importance. The scale may well attach equal weights to

such diverse matters as teacher absence, teacher participation in professional organizations, teacher knowledge of
his subject matter, and the teacher's ability to get along
well with students and peers.
3. Many rating scales have very low levels of reliability and
validity.

PERFORMANCE COMPARED TO JOB DESCRIPTIONS

A detailed job description should list all major tasks to be
performed by the individual employee. In practice, however, most
job descriptions are written with groups of employees in mind.
That is, one job description may be written for an elementary
principal, a typist or a maintenance worker; and the same job
description is then applied to all individuals who are assigned to
that employee classification. Further, most job descriptions do not
weight the relative importance of the tasks listed. If job descriptions are developed by analysis of the work performed by each
individual, coupled with the agreed upon major tasks to be
accomplished, they can serve as useful evaluative instruments.
Evaluations can, thus, be meaningfully conducted by a comparison
of the employee's performance to those duties, responsibilities and
tasks listed in the job description.

Advantages:

1. Job descriptions let the employee know which tasks he is
expected to perform. Therefore, the parameters within
which he is to be evaluated are clear to him.
2. Job descriptions eliminate overlapping responsibilities and
clarify role expectancies.
3. Job descriptions, if written for the total staff, provide a
check of complete district wide tasks to be performed, and
they assure that important tasks are not missed because of
a lack of written direction. This approach assists in
evaluation of a total staff's performance.

Disadvantages:

1. Job tasks change over time and the written job description
may not be rewritten to reflect the change of tasks.
2. Development of a comprehensive set of job descriptions is
a costly and time consuming activity. The continuous

updating of job descriptions causes a great expenditure of human energies.

PERFORMANCE COMPARED TO
STATED BEHAVIORAL OBJECTIVES

The writer believes that the use of clearly stated behavioral objectives that are subject to measurement, coupled with the types of observational instruments mentioned in the anthology that was edited by Simon and Boyer[3], hold the greatest promise for creative and objective evaluative systems in the immediate future. Examples of behavioral objectives and their usage in evaluations of various staff categories will now be presented.

A behavioral objective is a statement of terminal behavior that can be measured and compared to the criterion or standard that is stated. This allows for absolute measurement; and, thereby, evaluation can be accomplished. Behavioral objectives can be written for students, teachers and all types of employee groups. Behavioral objectives can be written for the cognitive, affective and psychomotor domains.

SPECIFIC EXAMPLES OF BEHAVIORAL OBJECTIVES

1. *A student objective in the cognitive domain* might be stated as: At the end of eight weeks of instruction John Jones, a 1st grade student, will be able to successfully read a random selection from the 1st grade reader ON TOP OF THE HILL with a minimum of three oral reading errors and with a comprehension score of at least 85% on the standardized test provided with the text. The individual student's objective states which behavior is expected, the situation in which the behavior is to be observed, how measurement is to occur, the time needed to bring about the expected behavior and the minimal level of acceptable performance. Individualized student objectives and student group objectives are very important tools in the evaluation of teacher effectiveness.

2. *A student objective in the affective domain* might be: After completion of a course in contemporary literature

---

[3]Simon, Anita and Boyer, E. Gil, *Mirrors for Behavior*. Philadelphia, Penn.: Research for Better Schools, Inc., January, 1968.

Mary May, a 12th grade student, will demonstrate her appreciation for such literature by reading at least six more contemporary literature volumes than she did in the previous four-month-period as measured by her free selection of books from the school library.

3. *A student objective in the psychomotor domain* might be: After Jimmy James, a 10th grade student, has completed the first week of typing class he will have reached a level of typing skill that, when presented a randomed scattered listing of the alphabet on a mimeographed sheet, he will be able to type a minimum of 95% of the letters in the proper alphabetical order without looking at the keyboard.

4. *A final yearly objective for a class* of 25 fourth grade students in the area of reading might well be: After one year of reading instruction a minimum of 85% of the students will display a minimum of 14 months of growth in overall reading achievement as measured by the Gates Standardized Reading Battery.

The reader certainly needs seriously consider the evaluation of accomplishment of such student behavioral objectives when attempting to evaluate teaching effectiveness. Behavioral objectives can also be stated for many tasks performed by various employee groups. Examples of performance objectives for various staff categories will now be presented:

1. A four man grounds crew will plant 100 maple trees in a two day period at the locations provided on a sketch drawn by the superintendent of buildings and grounds.

2. All 25 teachers in X Elementary School will take a 12 week in-service course in proper media usage. At the end of the 11th week all teachers shall demonstrate their ability to properly operate a tape recorder, movie projector and video tape recorder by successfully playing a tape, running a film and making a video recording. Further a minimum of 20 teachers, after the 12th week of instruction, shall demonstrate their proficiency by producing a 5 minute film strip and showing said film strip to the total staff.

3. Six weeks after the beginning of the school year the

director of personnel services shall submit to the super-intendent of schools a listing of all employees by age, sex, experience, educational level, staff category and building assignment.

4. The major yearly performance objectives for the district's curriculum coordinator could well be those listed below. Interim objectives, based upon the yearly objectives, could then be established with different time periods established for various stages of completion.

   a. The district curriculum coordinator shall develop a five year curriculum study plan which encompasses every subject area and which will be submitted in writing to the board of education by June 15th.

   b. He shall organize and conduct in-service courses in the areas of multi-media usage and the writing of behavioral objectives which will enroll a minimum of 39% of the teaching staff during the course of the 1971-1972 School Year.

   c. He shall organize a curriculum advisory committee in the area of mathematics that shall develop learning activity packets covering the content of a one semester course in matrix mathematics. The complete set of packets to be delivered to all buildings by May 30th.

5. The major yearly objectives for a group of employees can be demonstrated by the following examples:

   a. The district's maintenance staff shall repair all school building roofs during the current school year. Interim objectives could include the repair of the senior high roof, utilizing 3 men, by October 1st, could include the repair of the junior high school's roof, using 4 men for a one week period, by May 15th, and so forth.

   b. One hundred classrooms shall be repainted by a crew of six men over a period of 50 days. Interim objectives could be stated by setting a weekly quota, beginning on July 1st, of a minimum of ten classrooms.

   c. The maintenance staff will place new desks tops on 300 desks in B Elementary. Interim objectives, with qualifications as to the number of men assigned and the number of man hours to be devoted to the task could be developed.

The examples given above should provide the reader with a clear realization of the approach to task analysis on a delineated behavioral bases; and with a recognition of the implication of this approach to creative and objective staff evaluation. This discussion of behavioral objectives will be terminated with an outline of the process to be followed in developing a total process of evaluation by objectives. Although the example is that of evaluating teacher effectiveness, the same process could be modified and used for the purpose of evaluating any employee group.

Step I—Student needs are identified by the teacher by use of observation, standardized testing and anecdotal records. This process is to be followed in identifying the needs of each student and in identifying the needs of the entire class.

Step II—Based on the needs that have been identified, individual and group behavioral objectives are established. The objectives so developed need include long term and interim objectives.

Step III—The activities, processes, materials of instruction and instructional strategies are to be determined. Of course, these factors and/or approaches may need be modified during the course of the year.

Step IV—Techniques of periodic and long term observation and measurement need be determined. The techniques might include standardized testing, anecdotal records, observational recordings and numerous other instruments and techniques.

Step V—The preplanned activities are put into practice and observations are made. Video and audio recordings, as well as other standardized data gathering instruments, will prove valuable at this stage.

Step VI—This is the stage at which the data collected in stage V are analyzed. This stage permits assessment of the degree of achievement attained towards the stated behavioral objectives.

Step VII—The final stage of the process should involve the establishment of new objectives, the modification of objectives previously stated and the development of additional instruction techniques.

Of course, many of these steps could be utilized at the same time as they are applied to each student within the class. Certainly such an approach will permit the evaluator to assess the relative performance level of the teacher on the basis of clear cut statements of student objectives.

There are advantages and disadvantages in the utilization of behavioral objectives as a means to staff evaluation. The major advantages and disadvantages associated with the use of behavioral objectives are:

Advantages:

1. Items to be evaluated are stated in clear terms that are measurable.
2. Items to be evaluated are specific and behavioral, have a minimal level of acceptability, have a terminal date, and possess a delineated means of measurement.
3. Behavioral objectives enhance the degree of objectivity present in the evaluations.
4. Behavioral objectives, when applied to the teaching act, permit evaluation by means of student achievement. Thereby, the consumer's production can become an important factor in staff evaluation.
5. Behavioral objectives permit the evaluation of the total task, sub tasks, individual objectives and interim objectives.

Disadvantages:

1. A large amount of money and time need be devoted to staff training in order that they become proficient in stating their objectives in behavioral terms that are measurable.
2. Many individuals overemphasize the cognitive objectives and give very little thought to those which are affective and psychomotor in nature.
3. It is very difficult and time consuming for an employee or a supervisor to develop a comprehensive list of behavioral objectives.

4. Many complex duties are very difficult, it not impossible, to state in behavioral terms.

CRITERIA TO BE UTILIZED IN ACCOMPLISHING
THE TOTAL EVALUATIVE PROGRAM

Various types of criteria need be considered by the local district's committee that is charged with the responsibility of devising a comprehensive scheme of staff evaluation. Some criteria can be stated as absolutes and other criteria may permit great flexibility.

Absolute Criteria:

Absolute criteria should include such variables as health, knowledge, skills, attendance and ability to get along with others. Minimal standards, below which the employee is considered unsatisfactory, need be established for various staff assignments. For example, a custodian who has a chronic back ailment may not be able to perform the heavy tasks expected of all persons assigned to that job category; a teacher who is consistently tardy and causing his 1st period class of students to be deprived of a great deal of instructional time may not be considered satisfactory; a cook who does not have sufficient skill in the conversion of standardized recipes to those which will feed 500 youngsters may not be considered satisfactory; a cleaner who has no knowledge as to which wax to apply to different types of floor textures may not be considered satisfactory; a teacher who is assigned to a teaching team and who possesses a pugnacious attitude with all his co-workers may not be considered a satisfactory employee. Such absolute standardized criteria need be delineated, and they, in and of themselves, may be sufficient cause to judge an employee undesirable. The same employee, however, may rate very high on all other variables, and the decision would still need be one of an unsatisfactory judgement.

It need be stressed that these absolute variables should be located, whenever possible, during the employee's probationary period of employment. An employee with a lack of knowledge or skill may well be made satisfactory by providing him with on-the-job training which will correct the deficiency. The employee who has a health problem that restricts his job performance in one job category may be shifted into another job category in which he may perform in a very satisfactory manner. For example, the custodian with the chronic back ailment might well make an excellent night watchman. The evaluator and the employer owe their employees any consideration possible, within reason, in attempting to make an unsatisfactory employee into one who can perform in an acceptable manner.

Comparative Performances:

Another criterion which should be considered for inclusion in the district's evaluative program is that of comparing the individual and his performance level with that of other individuals assigned to the same job classification. Flexible standards of performance can be developed for sub-tasks, or a norm of production can be established as the basis for comparison.

A sub-task norm for all bakers could be established such as 220 loaves of bread are to be baked in a high-intensity oven in a four hour period. Those bakers not achieving the norm would be rated inadequate, those achieving a range between 210 and 230 loaves could be rated adequate, and those achieving a production greater than 230 loaves could be rated better than adequate.

A cleaner could receive a total evaluation of adequate if he completed a daily cleaning, up to established specification, of a square footage area of 18,000 square feet, with fewer than two complaints per week by the teachers who use the rooms. Also, his absenteeism rate could be compared to the norm for his employee group. Upon investigation, he may have had an unusual accident, and the explanation would cause the unsatisfactory rating in attendance to be waived.

The sub-task standards need to be given a weighting as to their importance in order to arrive at an overall standard upon which each employee is to be weighted. An abbreviated example will provide insights into the validity of sub-task weightings.

Weighted Sub-Task Standards for the Position of Secretary

Sub-task standard	*Weighting*
1. Retrieval of any single piece of information from her files in 3 or less minutes	5 points
2. Can take dictation at a minimum rate of 40 words per minute	10

3. Can type at a minimum rate of 45 words per minute with less than one error per page   10

4. Screens and answers a minimum of 75% of her administrator's mail   3

5. Places all scheduled appointments on her administrator's calendar and reminds him on a daily basis of his appointment schedule   1

6. Other

7. Other

Notes: A point total of 28 is deemed the minimal level of acceptable performance. The immediate supervisor can add up to double the amount of points in any single task, with the exception of numbers 4 and 5.

Comparison of Achievement to Stated Performance Goals:

Another criterion that needs to be carefully considered for inclusion into the total scheme of evaluation is that of the level of achievement as compared to stated performance goals. Probably the best performance goals are those set for an individual employee by the employee and his immediate supervisor. Examples of performance goals that are mutually developed by the employee and his supervisor are:

1. A principal and his supervisor agree that he shall, by December 1st, have at least five teachers agree to permit a one half hour reading lesson dealing with structural analysis skills committed to video tape, and these tapes shall be evaluated for use in a staff in-service program dealing with simulation activities.

2. The secretary and her immediate supervisor agree that she is to increase her typing speed by five words per minute, without increasing her number of errors, within a six-month period.

3. The superintendent of buildings and grounds and the superintendent of schools agree that the superintendent of building and grounds shall present a five-year paint schedule, involving every classroom in the school district, by the end of the current school year.

It is obvious that such mutually agreed upon goals are those of relatively high priority, and they are measurable after an agreed upon period of time. Such performance goals are of great importance in evaluating the performance of an individual employee on items of high priority.

Criteria Based Upon Student Achievement:

One very important element to be included in the evaluation of an individual teacher and of the production of the total teaching staff is the achievement of the end product of instruction—the students. Student achievement can be measured over time by conducting follow-up studies on the accomplishments of the school's graduates, by measuring the achievement of individual students and groups of students on clearly stated behavioral objectives, and by an analysis of student standardized test scores.

The measurement of the success of the school's graduates in college or in the work world provide a good indice of large group and long term achievement. Although these data are useful, those conducting the evaluation must be mindful of the fact that numerous intervening variables have had their effect over a long period of time, and many of these variables are beyond the control of individual teachers and of the total school district's influence.

Evaluation of individual and group achievements of students by means of behavioral objectives has been discussed earlier in the chapter. Suffice it to say that this approach to teacher evaluation should be carefully considered for inclusion in any plan of teacher evaluation.

Teacher evaluation by use of student scores on standardized achievement tests is one method that should probably be incorporated as a portion of the total evaluation scheme. The evaluator, however, must be cognizant of the fact that standardized tests normally measure only the areas of information retained and skills; they do not deal with attitudes, values, appreciations and other important outgrowths of instruction. Over-reliance on standardized test scores many also cause a decrease in teacher effectiveness, because low scores may cause the teacher to teach for the test. Finally, pupil achievement is due to many factors including the instructional environment provided by teachers who had the students in prior years.

Four

ESTABLISHING THE GOALS
AND PROCEDURES FOR A
SYSTEM OF TEACHER EVALUATION

This chapter and Chapter 5 will present practical examples of types of activities that must be undertaken in developing a comprehensive program of evaluation for the teaching staff. The major points to be discussed are: (1) Programming the goals, (2) Detailing the procedures, (3) Arriving at the techniques to be employed, (4) Deciding on the personnel to do the evaluations, and (5) Planning to evaluate the evaluators and the program of evaluation established.

PROGRAMMING THE GOALS

The initial step in the development of a scheme for teacher evaluation is that of devoting a large amount of time with all individuals who are to be evaluated or who are to be held responsible for conducting evaluations in dialoging the goals to be achieved. In a district where evaluation procedures have been carried on at a low level of sophistication or in a district where the staff is not accustomed to evaluation an interim plan of evaluation may have to be devised. For instance, a scheme based upon technical evaluative tools of classroom interaction or one which requires each teacher to write behavioral objectives for each student and for each class of students may be too dramatic a change for the staff. An interim plan could be made operational while the ultimate plan could be developed and sold for future use.

A reasonable set of goals, stated as underlying beliefs and general objectives, could assist in the development of the interim scheme of evaluation as well as help in providing direction for the more sophisticated, ultimate plan of evaluation. A listing of such statements of goals might well be stated as follows:

Underlying Beliefs

The evaluative responsibility of all employees must be geared to the maximization of a positive educational environment for children and youth. In order to accomplish this goal, the various aspects of this educational environment need be stated in behavioralistic terms that are measurable.

Each teacher has his own style of work, his own unique capabilities and his own strengths and weaknesses. District objectives, building level objectives and individual teacher's objectives, once clearly stated, allow for this individuality and provide the basis for evaluation of an individual teacher and a group of teachers.

Although many purposes are served by an evaluation program, the paramount purpose of an evaluation must be to assist the individual teacher in providing a high quality education for his students by continually improving the achievement towards the valid objectives of the district, the building level, the subject area, the grade level and the individual teacher and his students.

It is further realized that an interim scheme of evaluation may have to precede evaluation by means of concise behavioral objectives. The interim scheme will allow for necessary in-service activity, and it will provide the necessary time period during which all employees will feel comfortable with the process of evaluation developed on a behavioral basis.

General Objectives

The following general objectives must be considered prerequisites to any scheme of evaluation that is finally operationalized:

1. The evaluation scheme must be continuous and long-term, and it need include pre-employment evaluation for selection purposes, evaluation during the probationary period, a key evaluation for the period during which a tenure employment decision need be made, evaluation after tenure has been granted and evaluation, of an exit interview type, when the teacher is leaving the local school system.
2. The achievement of individual students and the total student body must be within an acceptable achievement range.
3. The evaluator and the evaluatee must know the objectives and must base the evaluation upon measurement of these objectives.
4. The use of evaluative data must be geared to the improvement of the staff member towards achieving the objectives.
5. The evaluative process must provide for detailed and regularized input and output informations that are available to both evaluator and evaluatee.
6. The evaluator has the obligation to compliment staff members in the areas of strengths and to assist them in obtaining help in their areas of weakness.
7. The evaluative process should be made as objective as practicable, but should include subjective data when such data are helpful.
8. The evaluative process should include the recipients (the students), co-workers, administrators and others who, from time to time, may serve as a positive outside auditing source.
9. The evaluative process should strongly stress self-evaluation as the basic building block.
10. A total program of evaluation must change as to purpose and over time. There is no *one* method of evaluation that fits all staff members over time.
11. A total program of evaluation shall have the following purposes:
    a) Assisting the individual staff member in improving his functions and in achieving stated objectives.

b) Communicating the performance expectations and the degree to which the individual staff member is achieving the expectations.

c) Assisting in the most appropriate assignment of staff.

d) Permitting administrative decisions to be more objective as to initial employment and tenure.

e) Providing a comprehensive cumulative personnel file, with accessibility guaranteed the staff member and the administration, which will develop the confidence of both parties.

f) Providing a feedback mechanism whereby the employees being evaluated can periodically assist in evaluation and modification of the system of evaluation.

DETAILING THE PROCEDURES AND
ARRIVING AT THE TECHNIQUES TO BE EMPLOYED

Once the goals of a program have been agreed upon, the decisions as to which procedures and techniques are to be incorporated into the evaluative scheme that is to become operational will occupy many hours of the planning staff's time. These procedural and technical decisions will need be made for: (1) pre-employment evaluations, (2) evaluations during the probationary period, (3) evaluations during the tenured period, and (4) evaluations at the termination of employment.

Pre-employment Evaluation

The selection of the types of staff members to be employed is a very important aspect of the total staff evaluation program. A thorough selection process can greatly enhance the probability of the individual teacher arriving with the types of specific educational and experiential backgrounds necessary for success at the local district level. Districts do differ in the types of staff characteristics desired, and careful attention to this fact will allow the evaluators to spend a much greater percentage of their time on the positive aspects of assisting good teachers to improve. The negative situation, that of compiling evidence of the teacher's inability to achieve the minimal standards of acceptability, can be greatly diminished if not completely eliminated.

A district's staff may feel that male teachers need be hired for the elementary grades, that it is important to have an age, sex and teaching experience balance at each grade level and within each individual school building. Also, the district's staff may decide what various institutions provide differing philosophical approaches to the teaching act, and a balance of philosophies might be considered important to the overall staffing constellation. Finally, if the teaching supply is sufficient, the importance of selecting excellent candidates who have been trained in team teaching, individualized instruction and other techniques needs be given weight; and the secondary assignments for such activities as yearbooks, athletics, cheerleading and other activities may be given consideration in the selection of candidates. If co-curricular activities are considered an important and integral part of the total educational experiences offered students, the staffing for these activities must not be left to chance. A few examples of how this data can be used in evaluating the total staff patterning will now be presented.

The district employs four teachers of aphasia. All four are female, and they are all graduates of a single university which specializes in the use of a technique that isolates these children from all outside stimuli. Isolation booths are present in each self contained classroom, the shades are continually drawn, no student work is displayed on the bulletin board and the students are not permitted to eat lunch in the school cafeteria. One teacher is leaving the staff to get married. She is moving to a different geographical location with her husband. The staff decides that some youngsters in the aphasic program would benefit from male teacher contact, and a different university is now providing an instructional training approach that assumes limited and controlled stimuli and assumes that pupil contact needs be built into the instructional program and increased over time. If the supply of candidates is sufficient, the type of individual to be hired is rather clear.

The senior high's social science department employs 20 teachers, all of whom are males and beyond 35 years of age. The junior high's staff, on the other hand, has 15 teachers, 10 of whom are females with less than 5 years of teaching experience. The staff agrees that a balance in terms of sex, age and years of experience is important. Besides attempting meaningful staff transfers among the existing staff, the new employees should be selected on the basis of the staff variables which are desired. This selection, of course, assumes a sufficient number of candidates to allow the selection to be made from candidates that are well-qualified and fairly equal on the other variables of training, experience and so forth.

The school housing the primary grades of the school district has recently decided to go into a completely ungraded, levels approach to instruction. This decision means that there will no longer be decisions made on the basis of kindergarten, first and second grades; but, rather, decisions will be based upon the completion of some 64 levels of performance throughout a flexible time period which may vary from three to five years. The key is individual student performance on the basis of cognitive, affective and psychomotor objectives which have been developed on the basis of the student's individual needs.

In selecting new staff members for this particular school building it is crucial that those individuals who have had educational training and/or actual teaching experience with this specific approach to instruction be given preference over other excellent teaching candidates who do not possess these background experiences. Thought given to these variables will allow the new teacher to feel much more comfortable with the instruction mode; will allow, immediately, better student instruction; will save much in-service cost and will enhance the chances for a teacher performance that will be deemed acceptable based on the district's minimal standards of performance.

With a high supply and low demand factor functioning attention can be given to the selection of staff members who are capable of handling important secondary assignments. For example, the district's decision makers have felt for a long time that a co-curricular activity should be added in the area of synchronized swimming. No one on the current staff is capable of sponsoring this activity; and, therefore, this offering has not been made available to the student body. For the next school year, 108 staff vacancies have been noted. The selection staff realized that, currently, there is a large oversupply of teachers in the areas of physical education, English and social science. Therefore, they advertize in the list of vacancies which is sent to all university placement offices the fact that preference is to be given in the areas of physical education, English and social science to candidates who also have the ability to sponsor synchronized swimming organization.

From the above examples, the reader can see the reasons for building into the total staff evaluation program a means of carefully pre-screening all available teaching candidates for the prime and secondary assignments to be assumed. If instructional programs are considered important enough to offer the students of the local school district, evaluation of the staff, on a pre-screening and continuous basis, is mandatory.

A simplified form to be used in data collection of staff characteristics could be developed; and summaries by buildings, grade levels and subject and other areas of training and/or assignment would be made readily accessible to those charged with the responsibility of hiring to achieve a staffing balance. An example form is presented in Figure 4-1.

SUMMARY OF PROFESSIONAL STAFF CHARACTERISTICS AS OF JUNE, 19 _ _

Teacher's Name	Building Assigned	Grade or Subject Area	Sex	Age	Number years experience within district	Number years experience outside district	Total years experience	Degrees received and date(s) granted	Institutions from which degrees were received	Major areas of academic preparation	Minor areas of academic preparation	Co-curricular areas qualified to sponsor	Areas of certification
1.													
2.													
3.													
4.													
Etc.													

Figure 4-1

A separate summary sheet could be used for new employees, and comparisons to the summary of total staff characteristics would allow one to determine how well the staffing voids were filled. The basic data collected could also be analyzed by building, grade level, subject areas and so forth; and means, medians, modes and ranges could be determined. All of these types of subsequent analysis would prove helpful to the decision makers dealing with the problems of total staff evaluation and balance.

Probationary and Tenured Evaluations

Once the teaching candidates have been screened and selected, the staff must immediately turn its attention to the procedures and techniques to be employed in the continuous evaluation of the total teaching staff. Example procedures and forms will now be presented.

A simplified procedural and time schedule for an interim program of total evaluation development that will permit the long term program development to continue as a parallel activity might be as shown in Figure 4-2. This particular procedure indicates the forms to be used, the types of individuals who are to perform the evaluations and the future need for a more sophisticated proto-type evaluation to be developed.

Once the procedural and time schedule has been agreed upon, the actual tools to be utilized need be developed. Of course video and audio tapes as well as various types of classroom behavioral observation systems could be utilized. For purposes of this discussion, however, a form to be completed by the teacher for the purpose of listing his priority goals is presented. Other forms presented are: (1) a teacher self evaluation form, (2) a form to be used by the principal in evaluating a teacher, and (3) a summary form to be completed by the building principal which provides necessary information for the use of central office personnel.

Although example forms are not presented in this discussion, forms using parallel questions to most of those listed on the teacher self evaluation and the principal's evaluation forms could be duplicated for use by teaching peers and by students. It is recommended, in fact, that this be done. The examples also provide an example of item weighting in the case of the teacher self evaluation form. This procedure must be given serious thought in the development of all forms. Finally, it should be noted that the two forms to be used by the administrator provide informa-

TEACHER EVALUATION – INTERIM – PROCEDURES AND TIME SCHEDULES

	Form Used	Date of Completion	Person Completing Form	To Whom Form Is Given	Comments
1.	Teacher Yearly Performance Objectives Form	By November 1st, yearly.	Classroom Tchr.	Principal	
2.	Teacher Self Evaluation Form	Prior to each conference with the principal	Classroom Tchr.	Principal	
3.	Student's Evaluation of Teacher Form	Second Week of January, yearly.	Each Student	Teacher	Teacher may wish to share the results with the Principal
4.	Teacher's Peer Evaluation Form	At any time when requested by another teacher.	Visiting Classroom Tchr.	Classroom Teacher Visited	The teachers may wish to share this evaluation with the principal.
5.	Administrator's Evaluation of Teacher Form	A minimum of ~ times yearly for probationary teachers and one per yr. for tenured teachers.	Principal and/or other administrator.	One copy to teacher, principal, & Dir. of Pers. Serv.	
6.	Yearly Principal's Summary of Recommendations of Teaching Staff Form	By March 1st, yearly.	Principal	Superintendent of Schools	
7.	Teacher Evaluation Prototype				To replace numbers 1, 2, 4 and 5 when fully developed.

Figure 4-2

tions that are required to make future administrative staff decisions and informations that are desirable for central office use.

In all cases, the forms presented are intended to be examples of interim evaluation procedures. The ultimate program may well be developed through means of detailed statements of behavioral objectives. These interim procedures, however, will permit a positive ongoing program while ultimate program decisions are being formulated.

Note: Also use the teacher's performance objectives for evaluation purposes.

Remember!

A final yearly recommendation must be presented to the Superintendent (copies to the Assistant Superintendent for Instruction and the Director of Personnel Services) by March 1st, yearly. In cases of staff members who began to teach at a time other than in September a final third year recommendation must be made no later than 90 days prior to the expiration of the teacher's probationary period. The Superintendent must legally notify the teacher in writing, not later than 60 days immediately preceding the expiration of the probationary period, if he is not to be granted tenure.

Taken as a total, the procedures and forms previously discussed can provide the nucleous of an interim proposal for teacher evaluation. Chapter 5 will develop the propositions to be considered when developing the more sophisticated and ultimate plan of teacher evaluation.

TEACHER YEARLY PERFORMANCE OBJECTIVES FORM

_____   _____
Name of Teacher   Date Form Completed

This form is to be completed in duplicate with one copy given to your
building principal and one copy retained by you. The principal's
copy should be presented by November 1st, yearly. Your statements will
be reviewed at a principal's conference as a part of the total evaluation procedure.

I expect to improve my teaching this year by accomplishing the following:
In the area of subject area knowledge:

    1. _____

       _____

    2. _____

       _____

In the area of techniques of instruction:

    1. _____

       _____

    2. _____

       _____

In the area of individualizing instruction:

    1. _____

       _____

    2. _____

       _____

Figure 4-3

In the area of clarification of instructional objectives for myself
and my students:

    1. _____

       _____

    2. _____

       _____

In the area of positive reinforcement of each student:

    1. _____

       _____

    2. _____

       _____

In the area of communication and cooperation with:

    A. Fellow Teachers:

    1. _____

       _____

    2. _____

       _____

    B. Building Administrators:

    1. _____

       _____

    2. _____

       _____

    C. Students

    1. _____

       _____

C. Students (continued)

2. _____

   _____

D. Parents:

1. _____

   _____

2. _____

   _____

E. Other School Employees (cafeteria, custodial, secretarial):

1. _____

   _____

2. _____

   _____

F. Teacher Aides:

1. _____

   _____

2. _____

   _____

G. District Level Participation in Future Planning:

1. _____

   _____

2. _____

   _____

In the area of other performance objectives (name):

1. _____

   _____

2. _____

   _____

Figure 4-3 (cont.)

TEACHER SELF EVALUATION FORM

This form is to be completed by the teacher and brought to the principals' conference after the principal has visited your class.

Name of Teacher	Date Form Completed

Area I - General Characteristics   Acceptable   Unacceptable

1. Appearance   / / /   / / /

2. Ability to get along with:

    Fellow teachers   / / /   / / /

    Parents   / / /   / / /

    Principal(s)   / / /   / / /

    Other Administrators   / / /   / / /

    Secretaries, custodians,   / / /   / / /
      cafeteria workers

    Teacher Aides   / / /   / / /

    Others   / / /   / / /

3. Health   / / /   / / /

4. Attendance Record   / / /   / / /

Area II - Specific Teaching Variables   Variable
                                             Weighting:

1. I feel my knowledge of my teaching area is:

        / 1 / 2 / 3 / 4 / 5 /   10
      Excellent   Poor

2. I feel my knowledge of individual student's interests, abilities
    and needs is:

        / 1 / 2 / 3 / 4 / 5 /   10
      Excellent   Poor

3. I believe that my goals and objectives for my lessons are to me:

        // 1 / 2 / 3 / 4 / 5 /   10
      Very Clear   Not Clear

4. I believe that my goals and objectives for my lessons are to
    my students:

Figure 4-4

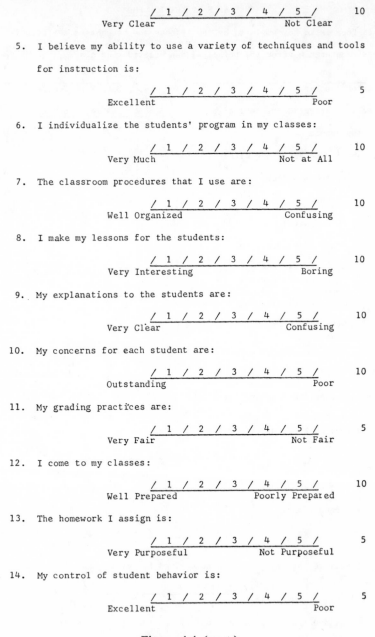

/ 1 / 2 / 3 / 4 / 5 /   10
Very Clear   Not Clear

5. I believe my ability to use a variety of techniques and tools

for instruction is:

/ 1 / 2 / 3 / 4 / 5 /   5
Excellent   Poor

6. I individualize the students' program in my classes:

/ 1 / 2 / 3 / 4 / 5 /   10
Very Much   Not at All

7. The classroom procedures that I use are:

/ 1 / 2 / 3 / 4 / 5 /   10
Well Organized   Confusing

8. I make my lessons for the students:

/ 1 / 2 / 3 / 4 / 5 /   10
Very Interesting   Boring

9. My explanations to the students are:

/ 1 / 2 / 3 / 4 / 5 /   10
Very Clear   Confusing

10. My concerns for each student are:

/ 1 / 2 / 3 / 4 / 5 /   10
Outstanding   Poor

11. My grading practices are:

/ 1 / 2 / 3 / 4 / 5 /   5
Very Fair   Not Fair

12. I come to my classes:

/ 1 / 2 / 3 / 4 / 5 /   10
Well Prepared   Poorly Prepared

13. The homework I assign is:

/ 1 / 2 / 3 / 4 / 5 /   5
Very Purposeful   Not Purposeful

14. My control of student behavior is:

/ 1 / 2 / 3 / 4 / 5 /   5
Excellent   Poor

Figure 4-4 (cont.)

15. My classroom assignments are:

$$/\ 1\ /\ 2\ /\ 3\ /\ 4\ /\ 5\ /\qquad 10$$

     Reasonable and Clear   Unreasonable
                                   and Confused

16. My students treat me with:

$$/\ 1\ /\ 2\ /\ 3\ /\ 4\ /\ 5\ /\qquad 5$$

     Respect   Disrespect

17. I would rank myself, compared to other teachers, as:

$$/\ 1\ /\ 2\ /\ 3\ /\ 4\ /\ 5\ /\qquad 0$$

     Outstanding   Poor

Note: All 10 point weightings receive 2 points   Total
per interval, all 5 point weightings receive 1.   Weighting = _____

Area III - Overall Statements

1. I believe that my singlemost strength is _____

   _____

   _____

2. I believe that my singlemost weakness is _____

   _____

   _____

3. I believe I can best improve my teaching by (Place an "X" by the
   statements you feel best describe your feelings):

     More concise instructional objectives   _____

     Greater individualization of students' programs   _____

     Clearer explanations   _____

     Greater individual student participation   _____

     Clearer goals   _____

     Clearer assignments   _____

     More teacher assistance to individual students   _____

     Greater use of interesting teaching methods   _____

     Greater use of multi-media materials   _____

     Better teacher preparation   _____

Fairer grading practices   _____

Greater concern for individual students   _____

Better control of student behavior   _____

Better teacher preparation of subject matter   _____

Better teacher preparation of teaching techniques   _____

Others (name):

_____   _____

_____   _____

_____   _____

_____   _____

_____   _____

4. I believe I could best be helped in improving my teaching by:

Taking a course in writing behavioral objectives   _____

Taking a course in the use of media   _____

Visiting other teachers who do an excellent job   _____

Having my classroom lessons periodically videotaped
and reviewed by myself and another teacher or
principal or other (name):   _____

_____

_____

_____

_____

_____

Figure 4-4 (cont.)

ADMINISTRATOR'S EVALUATION OF TEACHER FORM

_____   _____
Evaluator's Signature   Date of Evaluation

I have reviewed this evaluation and have received a signed copy for
my personal use.

_____   _____
Teacher's Signature   Date of Receipt

I wish to be re-evaluated by another administrator.
(Check correct box):   ＿＿／   ＿＿／
                                         Yes   No

Directions: This form is to be made out in triplicate by the principal

             or other administrator completing the evaluation. One

             copy is to be given to the teacher, one copy is to be kept

             in the principal's file on the teacher, and the third

             copy is to be sent to the Director of Personnel Services

             for filing in the teacher's district personnel file.

Area I - General Characteristics   Acceptable   Unacceptable

1. Appearance   ＿＿／   ＿＿／

    If unacceptable, state the specifics and determine and list a

    program to correct the problem: _____

    _____

    _____

2. Ability to get along with:

        Fellow teachers   ＿＿／   ＿＿／

        Parents   ＿＿／   ＿＿／

        Principal(s)   ＿＿／   ＿＿／

    Other Administrators   ＿＿／   ＿＿／

Figure 4-5

2. Ability to get along with: (continued)

    Secretaries, custodians and

       cafeteria workers   ▱   ▱

    Teacher Aides   ▱   ▱

    Others   ▱   ▱

    If unacceptable, state the specifics and determine and list a

    program to correct the problem: _____

    _____

                                       Acceptable   Unacceptable

3. Health   ▱   ▱

    If unacceptable, state the specifics and determine and list a

    program to correct the problem: _____

    _____

                                       Acceptable   Unacceptable

4. Attendance Record   ▱   ▱

    If unacceptable, state the specifics and determine and list a

    program to correct the problem: _____

    _____

Area II - Specific Teaching Variables

1. I feel this teacher's knowledge of his teaching area is:

           / 1 / 2 / 3 / 4 / 5 /
           Excellent   Poor

2. I feel this teacher's knowledge of his individual student's

    interests, abilities and needs is:

           / 1 / 2 / 3 / 4 / 5 /
           Excellent   Poor

Figure 4-5 (cont.)

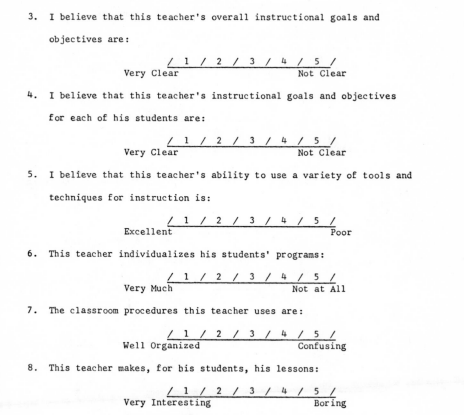

3. I believe that this teacher's overall instructional goals and objectives are:

/ 1 / 2 / 3 / 4 / 5 /
Very Clear   Not Clear

4. I believe that this teacher's instructional goals and objectives for each of his students are:

/ 1 / 2 / 3 / 4 / 5 /
Very Clear   Not Clear

5. I believe that this teacher's ability to use a variety of tools and techniques for instruction is:

/ 1 / 2 / 3 / 4 / 5 /
Excellent   Poor

6. This teacher individualizes his students' programs:

/ 1 / 2 / 3 / 4 / 5 /
Very Much   Not at All

7. The classroom procedures this teacher uses are:

/ 1 / 2 / 3 / 4 / 5 /
Well Organized   Confusing

8. This teacher makes, for his students, his lessons:

/ 1 / 2 / 3 / 4 / 5 /
Very Interesting   Boring

9. This teacher's explanations to his students are:

/ 1 / 2 / 3 / 4 / 5 /
Very Clear   Confusing

10. This teacher's concern for each student is:

/ 1 / 2 / 3 / 4 / 5 /
Outstanding   Poor

11. This teacher's grading practices are:

/ 1 / 2 / 3 / 4 / 5 /
Very Fair   Not Fair

12. This teacher comes to his classes:

/ 1 / 2 / 3 / 4 / 5 /
Well Prepared   Poorly Prepared

13. This teacher's homework assignments are:

/ 1 / 2 / 3 / 4 / 5 /
Very Purposeful   Not Purposeful

14. This teacher's control of student behavior is:

/ 1 / 2 / 3 / 4 / 5 /
Excellent   Poor

15. This teacher's classroom assignments are:

/ 1 / 2 / 3 / 4 / 5 /
Reasonable and Clear   Unreasonable and Confusing

16. This teacher's students treat him with:

/ 1 / 2 / 3 / 4 / 5 /
Respect   Disrespect

17. I believe this teacher, compared to other teachers, is:

/ 1 / 2 / 3 / 4 / 5 /
Outstanding   Poor

Area III - Overall Statements

1. I believe that this teacher's singlemost strength is: _____

_____

_____

2. I believe that this teacher's singlemost weakness is: _____

_____

_____

3. I believe that this teacher could best improve his teaching per-

formance by:

(Place an "X" by the statements that most closely describe your

opinions).

More concise instructional objectives   _____

Greater individualization of students programs _____

Clearer explanations   _____

Figure 4-5 (cont.)

Greater individual student participation   _____

Clearer goals   _____

Clearer assignments   _____

More teacher assistance to individual students   _____

Greater use of interesting teaching methods   _____

Greater use of multi-media materials   _____

Better teacher preparation   _____

Fairer grading practices   _____

Greater concern for individual students   _____

Better control of student behavior   _____

Better teacher preparation of subject matter   _____

Better teacher preparation of teaching techniques   _____

Others (Name):

_____

_____

4. I believe that this teacher could best be helped to improve his teaching by:

Taking a course in writing behavioral objectives   _____

Taking a course in the use of media   _____

Visiting other teachers who do an excellent job   _____

Having his classroom lessons periodically videotaped
    and reviewed by the principal or another teacher   _____

Other (Name):

_____

_____

5. I recommend that this <u>probationary teacher</u> (check appropriate boxes):

    /__/ Be continued on second year probation

    /__/ Be continued on third year probation

/ / Be reassigned to _____

/ / Be continued on probation if he completes the following
in-service training needs:

    a. _____

    b. _____

    c. _____

/ / Be terminated

6. I recommend that this <u>tenured teacher</u> (check appropriate boxes):

/ / Be reassigned to _____

/ / Be continued in his position if he completes the following
in-service training needs.

    a. _____

    b. _____

    c. _____

/ / Be considered for termination

Figure 4-5 (cont.)

<u>YEARLY PRINCIPAL'S SUMMARY OF RECOMMENDATIONS</u>
OF
<u>TEACHING STAFF FORM</u>

Directions: Each Building Principal shall duplicate this form and send
a listing of all teachers with his evaluation. He shall
also make his recommendations on all probationary teachers.
Said listing shall be presented to the Superintendent of
Schools by March 1st, yearly; and, in the case of those
teachers who began their employment during the school
year, at least 90 days prior to their employment anniver-
sary date.

Figure 4-6

Teachers on First Year Probation:

Name	Excellent	Above Average	Average	Below Average	Poor	Recommendation 2nd Year Pro-bation	Termi-nation
1.	☐	☐	☐	☐	☐	☐	☐
2.	☐	☐	☐	☐	☐	☐	☐
3.	☐	☐	☐	☐	☐	☐	☐

Etc.

Teachers Second Year Probation:

Name	Excellent	Above Average	Average	Below Average	Poor	Recommendation 3rd Year Pro-bation	Termi-nation
1.	☐	☐	☐	☐	☐	☐	☐
2.	☐	☐	☐	☐	☐	☐	☐
3.	☐	☐	☐	☐	☐	☐	☐

Etc.

Teachers Third Year Probation:

Name	Excellent	Above Average	Average	Below Average	Poor	Recommendation Tenure	Termi-nation
1.	☐	☐	☐	☐	☐	☐	☐
2.	☐	☐	☐	☐	☐	☐	☐
3.	☐	☐	☐	☐	☐	☐	☐

Etc.

Tenured Teachers:

Name	Excellent	Above Average	Average	Below Average	Poor
1.	☐	☐	☐	☐	☐
2.	☐	☐	☐	☐	☐
3.	☐	☐	☐	☐	☐

Etc.

Principal's Signature   Date of Completion

Five

DETAILING THE PROCEDURES AND TECHNIQUES FOR A SYSTEM OF TEACHER EVALUATION

This chapter picks up from Chapter 4 with a discussion of a teacher evaluation system utilizing behavioral objectives. Other points to be presented in this chapter are: (1) the use of the exit interview as a tool in the improvement of an overall program of teacher evaluation, (2) the means of deciding upon the personnel to perform teacher evaluations, and (3) the development of a scheme of evaluating the evaluators and the program of evaluation that has been established. The chapter terminates with a listing of selected bibliographical sources.

DETAILING THE PROCEDURES AND ARRIVING AT THE TECHNIQUES TO BE EMPLOYED

There are three major local tools that can be developed to use with teacher evaluations. These are job descriptions, job targets to be set by the individual teacher and statements of specific behavioral objectives. There are many other techniques that can be utilized in teacher evaluations. They are questionnaires, rating scales, video tapes, commercial tests of teacher competency and various commercial and research classroom observation techniques. The examples to be presented in this section will deal only with job descriptions and specific behavioral objectives. In both of these cases observation by an outside person will allow evaluation of specific items. The remaining devices and techniques may also be considered important tools in the total evaluative scheme, but job descriptions and a listing of behavioral objectives present the greatest challenge and work load to the local staff.

Job Description

An example of an elementary teacher's job description is presented in Figure 5-1. This job description lists major areas of assigned responsibility, and it lists some observable behaviors which the evaluator might use in conducting an evaluation of an elementary teacher. This is not the generalized type of job description so often seen in practice. This type of job description, coupled with a statement of the teacher's specific behavioral objectives for each student and the entire group of students assigned, will permit a rather detailed, objective evaluation to be conducted.

The weightings listed are examples. Each district would have to determine its own values and define the weightings for excellent, average, and so forth.

This job description demonstrates a technique which permits rather clear-cut measurement of accomplishment. This example is not all inclusive, nor is it necessarily considered a model. However, this approach should prove helpful in teacher evaluation, and the weighting provides both the teacher and the evaluator with comment as to the relative importance of each item.

Such job description could easily be converted to a rating scale. This procedure would permit the job description and the rating scale to become parallel tools, and this would be most helpful to the total evaluative scheme.

Behavioral Objectives

A behavioral objective is a statement of a terminal behavior that can be measured and compared to a stated criterion or standard. Behavioral objectives can be written for individuals and for groups of individuals. They can be long term, and interim objectives can provide short term and periodic measurements of progress towards the long term objectives.

Pauline Johnson

ELEMENTARY TEACHER JOB DESCRIPTION

Specific Duties and Responsibilities:		(Check one Column)			
Weight	Item	Achieved	Not Achieved	Not Applicable	Not Observed

Discipline 5 (1.) Shall be directly responsible for
the behavior of all students assigned.

a. The teacher shall clearly define
the expected limits of behavior to
all students assigned.   __ __ __ __

b. The teacher will be consistent
in the behavioral treatment of
b. students.   __ __ __ __

c. The teacher will devise activities
that will encourage self discipline
among his students.   __ __ __ __

d. The teacher, by his example, will
influence the desire of students to
self discipline themselves.   __ __ __ __

Instruction 30 2. Shall pre-plan the instructional
activities so as to allow for indi-
vidual differences among the students
assigned.

a. The teacher will use small group
and individualized instruction as
major modes of instruction.   __ __ __ __

b. The teacher will develop
behavioral objectives for each
student assigned.   __ __ __ __

Figure 5-1

c. The students will display abilities
to locate and use instructional materials
and supplies in carrying on their
learning tasks. ___ ___ ___ ___

d. The teacher will assign differentiated
homework to students. ___ ___ ___ ___

e. The students will spend differing
amounts of time on their instructional

e. tasks in order to achieve mastery. ___ ___ ___ ___

f. The students will be able to describe
their specific behavioral objectives and
display a knowledge of the means they
intend to use to accomplish the objectives. ___ ___ ___

g. The teacher will maintain a record
for each student which will reflect the
starting point of instruction, the strengths
and deficiencies of the student, the
objectives to be attained, the modes of
learning and the materials to be used
in attaining the objectives, and the
degree of success recorded, over time,
in achieving the objectives. ___ ___ ___ ___

h. The teacher demonstrated her assistance
to individuals as they attempt to resolve
learning difficulties. ___ ___ ___ ___

i. The teacher reinforces the individual
student by informing him in some manner
that he is important and his opinions and
problem solutions are important. ___ ___ ___ ___

j. The teacher modifies the instructional
program to take advantage of the skills of

Resource Personel

the ~~teacher aide~~ and of peer relationships

among students. ___ ___ ___ ___

Program
Development. 20   3. Shall develop ~~objectives~~ units for the instructional

program that can be ~~stated in measurable behav-~~ reused

~~ioral outcomes.~~ by other teachers.

a. The teacher will demonstrate the ability

units in Language Arts and in Env. St.
to write ~~behavioral objectives~~ for the

~~instructional program and for each student~~

~~assigned.~~ ___ ___ ___ ___

b. The teacher will demonstrate his/user

these units
of ~~behavioral~~ objectives with the class

and with each individual student assigned. ___ ___ ___ ___

Evaluation 20   4. Shall develop evaluation techniques that

are appropriate to the expected class and the

individual student's objectives. ___ ___ ___ ___

a. The teacher will use appropriate verbal

and non-verbal techniques in evaluating

student performance. ___ ___ ___ ___

administered
b. The tests ~~for each behavioral objective~~

will include measurement of (1) the levels of

cognition - knowledge, comprehension, application,

analysis, synthesis and evaluation, (2) the levels

of affection - receiving, responding, valuing,

organization and characterization, and (3) the

variables of psychomotor skills - frequency,

energy and duration. ___ ___ ___ ___

c. The teacher adjusts each student's program

based upon the evaluation data collected. ___ ___ ___ ___

Figure 5-1 (cont.)

d. The teacher provides students with

opportunities for self assessment.

e. *The teacher records all data in such a way that its interpretation is clear to all.*

Management 10 5. Shall arrange for the use of a variety of

teaching supplies, equipment and instructional material.

a. The teacher utilizes ~~the teacher aide~~ *the available resources to*

~~in the~~ prepar~~ation of~~ instructional materials that

are not commercially available. __ __ __ __

b. The teacher encourages students to use

the media ~~production center for the~~ *available to* development ~~of~~

tailor made instructional materials which serve

the individual student's purposes. __ __ __ __

c. The teacher has available, and the students

demonstrate the use of, video and audio tapes,

programmed learning materials, films, filmstrips,

high interest controlled vocabulary materials and

a variety of other instructional tools. __ __ __ __

Program Dev. 10 6. Shall correlate instruction with other instructional

areas when possible and desirable.

a. The teacher plans experiences that include

art, music and physical education in order to

demonstrate the interrelationships of the

curriculum. __ __ __ __

b. The teacher works with the science, math and

other curriculum specialists, *(consultants)* in planning the best

methods of achieving the needs of each pupil. __ __ __ __

c. The teacher calls for case conferences with *the principal, the vice-principal,*

the school nurse, the school psychologist, ~~the~~

~~elementary guidance counselor~~, the speech therapist

and other specialized personnel when a student

demonstrates a learning disability that he cannot

handle as a classroom teacher. __ __ __ __

Supervision   5   7.   Shall supervise students within and without the

classroom in accordance with the building regu-

lations established.

a. The teacher will be physically present in the

area to which his students are assigned. __ __ __ __

b. The students will demonstrate the manners

and modes of conduct that have been defined as

by the school staff.
acceptable by the district's staff. __ __ __ __

Supervision   5   8.   Shall take student attendance as legally

required and in the manner prescribed by the

attendance office.

omit {
a. The teacher will demonstrate his awareness that

attendance data is the auditing procedure for deter-

mining the appropriate amount of money to be alloted

to the district from the State. __ __ __ __

a. b. Information required for attendance reporting

will be accurately listed, and the office will

receive attendance reports on the days

indicated. __ __ __ __

Prof. Dev.   5   9.   Shall carry his share of professional duties

including those assigned by the ~~building~~ principal.

a. The teacher is seen by other staff members as

one who has a willingness to accept his share of

assignments. __ __ __ __

b. The teacher actively participates in

county-wide
~~district-wide~~ curriculum work and in other

activities intended to foster the students'

welfare. __ __ __ __

Supervision   4   10. Shall review fire drill and emergency

procedures with all students.

a. The teacher will block each exit at some

Figure 5-1 (cont.)

point in the year in order that the students will

become acquainted with the alternate routes of

escape to take in case of emergency. ___ ___ ___ ___

b. The teacher will keep a record of the time it

took for her class to flee the building, and he

shall continue emergency drills until an acceptable

time margin is accomplished. ___ ___ ___ ___

Management

2 11. Shall attend all faculty meetings and other

administrative meetings as requested by the principal.

a. The teacher is physically present at all meetings called

by the principal unless excused by the principal prior to

the meeting. ___ ___ ___ ___

Management

2 12. Shall be responsible for the assignment and care of instruc-

tional materials given to students and insures their return.

a. The teacher develops an inventory of all materials of

instruction. ___ ___ ___ ___

b. At the end of the year, the teacher informs the principal

of all materials not returned, of the condition of all materials,

and of the names of students who were assigned materials that

had not been returned. ___ ___ ___ ___

Total weighted points = 116 points

Assuming that teaching performance will be measured by the performance level achieved by the group of students assigned and by the performance of each student on his specific behavioral objectives, the process steps to be followed are:

Step 1. Determine the needs of the individual students and of the group of students by use of observations, anecdotal records, standardized tests or other means of data collection.

Step 2. Based on the identifiable needs, individual and group long-term objectives are written. This process includes answers to:

a. Who is to display the terminal behavior desired?

b. Under what conditions is the behavior to be observed?

c. What instructional strategies are to be used in achieving the objectives?

d. What amount of time is to be allowed for the development of the desired terminal behavior?

e. What is the desired minimal level of competency to be achieved?

f. Who is to monitor and measure the performance achieved?

g. What tools of measurement are to be used in assessing the performance level displayed? and

h. At what point of assessment shall the behavioral objectives be modified and/or new behavioral objectives written?

Step 3. After the long-term behavioral objectives have been written, a list of interim performance objectives need be developed. The same questions as those listed for long-term behavioral objectives need be answered in this step.

Step 4. A summary evaluative report of total progress towards long-term behavioral objectives is developed, and

Step 5. The entire process begins its recycling stage.

A partial listing of behavioral objectives for a group of students will now be presented, and a partial listing of behavioral objectives for a hypothetical student will also be given as an example of the total process of behavioral objective establishment.

Terminal Behavior Objectives for a Class of Students

Typical behavioral objectives for a fifth grade self-contained class of 25 students could well be:

1. Each student will be able to demonstrate listening skills by being able to analyze the major points of a general verbal discussion among a group of five pupils, by carrying out oral directions given by the teacher, and by analyzing the major points in the appropriate sequence of a lecture presented by an outside speaker. A minimum of 80% of

the members of the class will be able to demonstrate their ability to listen by repeating the directions, orally presented, to a science experiment; and by repeating the important points of a lecture on the historical background for present day racial problems in the United States. Measurement will be by observation of student oral discussions of the points and sequences made, by successfully carrying out the oral directions given, and by writing the major points and sequences of oral presentations.

2. In the area of physical education, 85% of the fifth grade boys and 90% of the fifth grade girls will demonstrate coordination skill development by being able to successfully demonstrate two successive foot to foot somersaults on a trampoline.

3. A minimum of 40% of all fifth grade students will demonstrate a positive attitude towards their instructional program by voluntarily selecting the option of attendance at the enrichment summer session offered by the school district.

4. Each student will demonstrate his knowledge of the base system of numeration by orally repeating and by writing a base 10 system in the mathematical language of base 2 and base 5. A minimum of 65% of the students will demonstrate their comprehension of bases by writing a conversion of the base ten system into a minimum of six additional bases.

5. A minimum of 78% of the students shall demonstrate their comprehension of the science concepts presented during the year by scoring a minimum of 90% correct answers on the pre-selected (name to be inserted) standardized test of fifth grade science comprehension. Also, no student shall register a score of less than 50% on this same test.

6. Many other very specific examples to be listed.

These examples illustrate cognitive, affective and psychomotor objectives. They also involve measurement by oral, written and physical performance means. Finally, they utilize measurement by observation, by teacher-made assignments and by standardized testing methodologies. Obviously, interim objectives could be developed for each of the terminal objectives listed, and measurement could be conducted at various time periods throughout the school year.

Terminal Objectives for a Single Student

The terminal objectives for a male fifth grade student who has displayed a rather "normal" pattern of needs determined from analysis of a prior collection of anecdotal, standardized testing and observational data, might well be as listed below. The examples are not meant to be comprehensive, and interim objectives and measurements would need be developed in a real life situation.

Objective #1. John will be able to demonstrate his ability to use structural analysis skills in reading by scoring a 90% correct score on the standardized fifth grade battery that was pre-selected (test to be named) in the section of the test dealing with the identification and proper usage of structural analysis clues. A 90% correct rate would translate into a score equivalency of 6th grade 2 months above the normed median.

Objective #2. John will successfully identify 98% of the homonyms, synonyms and antonyms provided on the two teacher-made tests provided as measurement instruments to be completed after completion of the learning activity packet assigned.

Objective #3. John will identify with 95% accuracy the (a) definition, (b) opposite meaning, (c) proper usage in three sentences, and (d) proper usage in a paragraph of selected words provided in context as outlined by Exercise A.

Objective #4. John will demonstrate his ability to understand structural and phonetic skills by orally stating and by writing the: (a) rules for words that double the final consonant before adding a suffix, (b) rules which apply to the final "e" before suffixes beginning with vowels and those beginning with consonants, (c) the rules for spelling contractions of two or more words. He shall also give a minimum of five examples of the application of each of these rules.

Objective #5. In the area of social science, John shall be able to demonstrate his understanding of the current civil rights problems in the United States by:

    (a) Relating orally or in written form a minimum of five historical events of importance to the civil rights movement.

    (b) Relating orally or in written form a minimum of three current civil rights cases that are now in the hands of the courts.

    (c) Writing a paper discussing his personal views on the topic of civil rights.

    (d) By listing examples of laws that were written to protect the rights of individual citizens. At least two laws must be explained in detail.

    (e) By telling or writing one example of how the federal, state and local governmental units have protected the civil rights of an individual or a group of individuals, and by receiving a minimal score of 85% correct on the end of the unit, teacher made test dealing with the areas discussed within the teaching and learning unit on civil rights.

Objective #6. Many other specific examples to be listed.

Behavioral objectives, such as the example group and individual objectives given, provide a detailed method of measuring the level of student performance on those specific skills, knowledges and attitudes that have been purposely built into the instructional program. Further, what better means does one have of evaluating the level of a teacher's proficiency than that of measuring the accomplishments of his pupils?

Exit Interview

The final stage of evaluation for any single employee takes place at the exit interview. Although many districts do not build in an exit interview for employees who are leaving, it is highly recommended that the local committee who is charged with the responsibility for the development of a total evaluation program give this serious consideration. For the individual staff member, this provides an opportunity to receive compliments for many fine performances, and it also provides a final opportunity to receive suggestions as to means of improving those areas in which improvement is still desirable. For the school district, it provides an opportunity to ask for answers to questions that will assist in the improvement of the total plan of staff evaluation in the future.

If an employee is convinced that he will not be identified and constructive suggestions are being solicited for the purpose of improving the future program of staff evaluation, valuable hints for improvement can be garnered by asking questions such as the following:

1. Do you feel that you received a sufficient number of visits for evaluative purposes? Why did you answer as you did?
2. Do you feel that the evaluations by your fellow teachers, by the principal, by your students and by the central office administrators were helpful? Which category of evaluators do you feel were the most helpful? Which were the least helpful?
3. Did you find that the video tapes of your teaching were helpful to you in the improvement of your teaching performance?
4. Was the method of writing behavioral objectives for your students helpful to you in improving your teaching performance? Did you feel that you were provided a sufficient amount of time in your daily and yearly schedule to write the behavioral objectives? Were you provided with a sufficient amount of in-service and on-the-job training to cause you to feel competent and comfortable when given the task of writing behavioral objectives?
5. When you and the persons assigned as evaluators located areas needing improvement in your performance, were you provided with sufficient help to allow you to improve? What type of help was provided? Are there other means of assistance that could have, or should have, been given you?
6. In what ways would you suggest that the total plan for evaluation in the school district be improved? Why have you answered in this way?
7. Many other valid questions could be included.

DECIDING ON THE PERSONNEL TO PERFORM TEACHER EVALUATIONS

Much discussion must precede a final decision as to which categories of personnel to include as evaluators of teachers. There are advantages and disadvantages to the inclusion of any single type of personnel category of evaluators. It is suggested that a combination of the various categories be carefully considered as the most constructive final answer for the local school district's total evaluation program.

The types of evaluators that need be considered are: (1) peers within the teaching staff, (2) students, (3) self evaluations, (4) lay residents, (5) outside paid consultants, (6) central office adminis- trators, and immediate administrative supervisors. Rather than repeat the major advantages and disadvantages of utilizing each category of evaluator at this point, the reader is referred to the rather complete listing of advantages and disadvantages that were previously presented in Chapter 2 of this book.

There are many advantages to be gained by the involvement of multiple categories of evaluators in the act of evaluating individual teacher's performances. The major advantage, of course, is that of presenting a check and balance system within the program of staff evaluation.

A model of multiple category of evaluator involvement, utilizing the tenure structure decided upon by the Godwin Heights Public Schools of Wyoming, Michigan, is shown in Figure 5-2. This model provides for self evaluations, evaluations by more than one teacher peer and evaluation by the building principal. The Godwin model also allows for the evaluation, upon request, of tenured teachers. Finally, this model permits a continuous review structure of the total evaluation process at the building and district levels; and the continuous evaluation of the process includes a review by board of education representatives, central administrative repre- sentatives and representatives of the teaching staff.

This structure, which is incorporated into the master contract that was signed by the board of education and the teachers' association, has operated in a discriminatory manner since the School Year 1966-1967. Although the great majority of Godwin Heights' teachers have received tenure appointments, a few have been forced to put in an additional year of probation and a few have not received tenure appointments. Finally, at least one tenured teacher was dismissed under this process even though a final ruling had to be rendered by the State of Michigan's Tenure Commission.

TENURE POLICY

THE GODWIN HEIGHTS EDUCATION ASSOCIATION
FOR
GODWIN HEIGHTS PUBLIC SCHOOLS

Definition: "Tenure is a system through which the best possible
               teaching staff is secured, developed and retained.
               It gives security to good teachers and provides an
               orderly method of dismissal of incompetent teachers."

Purpose: We firmly believe that tenure will provide better
               instruction for the children of the School District
               of Godwin Heights and will make teaching a more de-
               sirable profession because it will enable teachers
               to match in professional responsibility the privi-
               lege of the security it confers.

Authority: The Godwin Heights Board of Education has taken the
               following action: "That the Godwin Heights Board of
               Education recognizes the Godwin Heights Education
               Association as the official organization for the
               implementation of the Teacher Tenure Act in the
               Godwin Heights Public School System."

Introduction: We recognize the fact it is an administrative
               function to hire teachers.

               We believe it is of utmost importance that worthy
               teaching personnel be secured and retained on the
               staff.

               We believe that teachers are in an advantageous
               position to evaluate members of their own pro-
               fession and should actively help in this procedure.
               By assuming this responsibility we believe a more
               accurate evaluation will be obtained and admin-
               istrative decisions concerning teacher employment
               can be made more intelligently and with greater
               ease.

IN-SERVICE EVALUATION AND PROCEDURES OF TENURE POLICY

        It is equally important to develop an evaluation program to
measure the improvement and growth of the new teacher, and to
assure that constructive criticism will be administered in a beneficial, reasonable and just manner. It is necessary to have an instrument capable of informing a teacher new to the system with the tenure
policy and its operation in the Godwin Heights Public Schools.

        The following procedures shall serve as a guide for this
operation.

    I. Advisors to Teachers on Probation
        An advisor shall be appointed for each teacher on probation by
        his principal on or before the first day of each school year,
        or at the beginning of employment of the teacher.

Figure 5-2

The advisor assigned may be changed at any time by the principal at the request of either the advisor or the teacher on probation or at the discretion of the principal.

A. Qualifications of the Advisor
    1. The advisor must be a teacher on tenure status.
    2. Teach in same subject area or grade level, if possible.
    3. Advisor must be an active member of the Godwin Heights Education Association.

B. Duties of the Advisor
    1. Familiarize the teacher on probation with the traditions and policies of the Godwin Heights School System.
    2. Help teacher on probation adjust in his relationships with adult personnel in his building.
    3. Make himself available for counsel in instructional and disciplinary matters.
    4. Help in evaluation of teacher on probation through two class visitations per semester. The first visit should be at invitation of person to be evaluated. The second at pleasure of advisor. Purpose of the evaluation is to assist in the improvement of instructor and instruction.
    5. At no time should the advisor assume the position of being a supervisor of the classroom work of the teacher on probation, rather he should take the position of a friendly counselor offering constructive suggestions.
    6. Reports made by advisor to building tenure committee shall be in writing using the observation evaluation form adopted by the system tenure committee.
    7. The advisor is a non-voting member of building tenure committee unless elected to building tenure committee.
    8. Notify building tenure chairman immediately when aware that a written program of assistance is needed for teacher on probation.
    9. Participate in forming written program of assistance.

II. Building Tenure Committee

A. Membership of this committee shall consist of the following:
    1. Four teachers -- on tenure status and active members of the Godwin Heights Education Association.
    2. Building principal -- regardless of tenure status or his professional affiliations.
    3. The five committee members shall annually at their first meeting select a chairman from own group and a secretary.

B. Election of Committee Members
    1. By all building teachers who have tenure status. (Plurality vote)
    2. During first ten days of school.

C. Term of Office of Committee Members
    1. One member for one year.
        One member for two years.
        Two members for three years.
    2. As term expires succeeding elected member will serve for a three year term.

3. Vacancy -- term shall be filled by a tenure teacher
   elected by a plurality vote of building tenure teachers
   at a special meeting called by building chairman within
   ten (10) days after vacancy occurs.
4. Eligibility for re-election -- each member may serve
   consecutively two three-year terms.

D. When another unit not represented by a building tenure
   committee is added to the Godwin System, that building
   principal shall serve as temporary chairman to implement
   items A, B and C above.

E. Duties of Chairman of Building Tenure Committee
   1. Responsible for building tenure committee member
      elections. All nominations shall be made from the floor
      and those persons or person receiving the plurality vote
      shall be elected to the expired positions or position.
   2. Call at least two meetings of building tenure committee
      during each school year.
   3. Assign building tenure committee members to observe and
      evaluate teachers on probation. Evaluation form adopted
      by system tenure committee is to be used.
   4. Call meetings when requested by probationer, advisor,
      committee member, or building principal.
   5. During first three weeks of employment hold a meeting
      with all teachers (or teacher) on probation to inform
      them concerning tenure policies of the Godwin Heights
      School system.
   6. Schedule conference of teacher on probation, advisor,
      tenure visitor and principal when written program of
      assistance is needed.
   7. Show summary of evaluations to teacher if he is interested.
   8. Follow suggested "Calendar -- Evaluation for Teachers on
      Probation" recommended by system tenure committee.
   9. Prior to March 1, submit Building Tenure Committee
      Reports (Forms S) to Superintendent.
   10. Responsible for planning observation evaluations of
       teacher on tenure when requested.(See Building Tenure
       Committee, Item I., 4.)

F. Duties of Building Tenure Committee Secretary
   1. Write minutes of building tenure committee meetings to
      be filed in building tenure file.
   2. Prepare list of teachers on probation and their advisor
      for superintendent via system tenure chairman. This to
      be done after one week of employment.
   3. Complete Form S (Building Tenure Committee Report to
      Superintendent) for each teacher on probation. Copies
      to be filed shall be supplied to superintendent, build-
      ing principal (this copy accessible to chairman) and
      copy for teacher on probation.

G. Duties of Committee Members (Referred to as "tenure visitor")
   1. Each semester make one written observation evaluation of
      teacher on probation assigned to him or her. Use same
      evaluation form as advisor.
   2. Conference with teacher on probation after each obser-
      vation.
   3. Sign Building Tenure Committee Report to Superintendent
      and any additional reports regarding status of teacher

Figure 5-2 (cont.)

       on probation. These reports shall be considered advisory.
4. When necessary assist advisor and principal in making a
   written program of assistance in cases where teacher on
   probation needs additional help.
5. Make additional observations if deemed necessary by
   principal.

H. Duties of Principal
  1. Each semester make one written observation evaluation of
    teachers on probation.
  2. Conference with teacher on probation after each observation.
H. 3. Notify building tenure chairman immediately when aware
    that a written program of assistance is needed for teacher
    on probation.
  4. Participate in forming written program of assistance.
  5. Schedule conferences for each teacher on probation to
    meet with tenure committee to read, discuss, and sign
    Guiding Tenure Committee Report to Superintendent.
  6. Sign Building Tenure Committee Report to Superintendent
    and any additional reports regarding status of teacher
    on probation. These reports shall be considered advisory.
  7. Responsible for implementing the Godwin Heights Educa-
    tion Association Tenure Policy when representing a new or
    additional unit added to the Godwin Heights Public Schools.
  8. At discretion of tenure committee the building principal
    (in some unusual circumstances) may represent the tenure
    committe in the evaluation summary conference with the
    teacher on probation.
  9. May request observation evaluation by tenure committee
    of a teacher on continuing tenure.

I. Duties of Building Tenure Committee as a Whole
  1. Approach all procedures with professional attitude.
  2. Reports and data acquired by building tenure committee
    are confidential and shall be kept in the principal's
    office in a separate file. This file shall be avail-
    able at all times only to the principal, superintendent
    and building tenure chairman. Although he may not him-
    self examine his file, an individual teacher may request
    a review of his tenure dossier. Such records may be
    delivered through the building tenure chairman only upon
    written request from the individual involved. The
    building tenure chairman shall be responsible for the
    issuance of these records only to the system committee
    chairman, official Michigan Education Association
    representatives, or other legally authorized persons.
  3. As soon as teacher on probation attains tenure status
    and is placed on continuing tenure, the files are to
    be removed from building tenure committee's file and
    transferred to the principal's file. The building
    principal may remove materials he feels pertinent and
    necessary to complete the teacher's personal file, the
    remainder to be disposed of by the principal.
  4. Evaluation of tenure teacher will be made by the build-
    ing tenure committee only upon request by the Board of
    Education, administration, or if deemed necessary by the
    Godwin Heights Education Association. Upon completion
    of the evaluation the records are to be removed from the
    building tenure committee file and presented to the
    party requesting the evaluation.

III. Teacher on Probation

    A. Procedures
       1. Invite advisor to observe sometime during first seven weeks of employment.
       2. Make one written self-evaluation each semester using evaluation form adopted by system tenure committee. This completed form is given to building tenure chairman at end of each semester.
       3. May request from the building principal at any time a change of advisor.
       4. A conference may be requested by teacher on probation with any or all of the following: advisor, tenure visitor, or principal.
       5. Attend the conference with tenure committee which will be planned for each teacher on probation. At this conference read, sign and discuss his or her Building Tenure Committee Report to Superintendent. Teacher may also see summary of observation evaluations if he or she so desires.
       6. After completing second year on probation teacher may be recommended by committee to be placed on continuing tenure or be placed on third year probation.
       7. When a third year probation is recommended it is the duty of teacher on probation to make a written request through the superintendent to the Board of Education for this additional year of probation.

IV. Teacher on Continuing Tenure

    A. A teacher on continuing tenure from another district beginning employment with the Godwin Heights Public Schools shall be _required_ by the Board of Education to serve one year as a teacher on probation.

V. System Tenure Committee

    A. Membership of this committee shall consist of the following members:
       1. System tenure chairman.
       2. Superintendent of Schools or Assistant.
       3. Member from Board of Education.
       4. Building Tenure Committee Chairman (Presently there are 5).
       5. Advisory members -- building principals, president of Godwin Heights Education Association.

    B. Election of System Tenure Chairman
       1. By tenure teachers on faculty before October first.
       2. Nominations will be made by building tenure committees.
       3. Nominees must be teachers having tenure status and be active members of Godwin Heights Education Association.
       4. Mechanics of election will be performed by Godwin Heights Education Association.
       5. Term of office two (2) years.
       6. Vacancy -- term shall be filled by tenure teacher elected by Association at its first meeting following resignation or retirement (or within 15 days a special election will be called by Godwin Heights Education Association Executive Board).

Figure 5-2 (cont.)

C. Duties of System Tenure Chairman
    1. Call meetings of system tenure committee.
        a. First meeting shall be first Wednesday in October
            for purpose of organization.
        b. Additional meetings may be called as need arises.
    2. Represent system tenure committee on Godwin Heights
        Education Association Executive Board as Tenure Chairman.
    3. Present to GHEA executive board recommendations for
        changes or additions of tenure policy, evaluation guides
        and forms. This to be done by April 20.

D. Duties of System Tenure Secretary
    1. Write minutes of system tenure meetings and send copies
        to:
        a. Committee members
        b. Building principals
        c. President Godwin Heights Education Association.
    2. Compile list of teachers on probation and their advisor.
        List alphabetically according to building assigned and
        send to superintendent.
    3. Notify committee members of meeting time and place.
        (Usually 3:30 to 4:30 P.M.; administration building
        conference room.)

E. Duties of Superintendent as Member of System Tenure Committee
    1. Have secretary complete for each teacher on probation
        the heading on Building Tenure Committee Report to
        Superintendent form to item RECOMMENDATIONS. Send these
        to Building Tenure Chairman.
    2. Represent the administration on system tenure committee.
    3. Interpret system tenure committee recommendations to
        administrators and Board of Education.
    4. Have secretary to administration process personnel
        files as changes in tenure status are approved by Board
        of Education.
    5. Notify secretary of Board of Education in writing con-
        cerning cases requiring third year probation. Secretary
        of Board notifies State Tenure Commission.
F. Duties of Board of Education Member to System Committee
    1. Interpret tenure policy and procedures recommended by
        system tenure committee to members of Board of Education.
    2. Interpret Board of Education recommendations to system
        tenure committee.

G. Duties of System Tenure Committee as a Whole
    1. Select a secretary to write meeting minutes. Copies are
        sent to ... see item V., C., 1.
    2. Compose all evaluation guides and forms to be used by
        advisors and tenure committees.
    3. Draw up a time schedule calendar for implementing tenure
        policy and procedures. This to be done each spring.
        Calendar is to be used by building tenure committees
        during the ensuing year.
    4. Review annually the tenure policy, all evaluation guides
        and forms. Also the time schedule calendar.
    5. Consider all matters which concern the entire school
        system in implementation of tenure policy.
    6. Recommendations for dismissal of tenure teachers may
        be considered by this body.

EVALUATING THE EVALUATORS AND THE PROGRAM
OF EVALUATION

It is meaningful to approach the evaluation of the evaluators by assessing the consistency of their evaluations over a lengthy period of time and by comparing their evaluations of specific employees to the evaluations of the same employees submitted by other evaluators. If, in the process, an evaluator is found to be consistently high or low in his evaluations compared to the district's norms, a corrective formula could be devised to correct an evaluator's consistent tendency to overestimate or underestimate as compared to the established norm. Finally, an evaluator who displays inconsistency in his evaluations over a period of time can either be trained by an individualized in-service approach to the problem, or he can be eliminated from the team that is held responsible for conducting the evaluations.

The best single means of identifying the quality of the system of evaluation is by determining whether or not the system works. Certainly, modifications to the system of evaluation need be made over a time period as over time needs change and changes take place in the skills needed to successfully operate a local instructional program. Examples of changes that have called for modification in the evaluation process are: (1) the introduction of team teaching, small group instruction, large group instruction, independent study and other modes of instruction, (2) the introduction of programmed materials, television lectures, computer assisted instruction and other changes, and (3) the initiation of programs of "new" math, MINNEMAST (a science and math combined approach), BSCS Biology, PSSC Physics, and numerous other structural approach changes.

There are two prime means of determining whether or not the total system of evaluation is working. The initial check can be made by permitting and encouraging the individuals who have been evaluated and the individuals who have conducted the evaluations to tell those in decision making roles whether or not they feel the system is fair, mechanically easy to administer, assists in identifying the individual employee's strengths and weaknesses and permits the development of more effective performance through job upgrading and in-service. The second check on whether or not the system works is one of determining whether or not the system allows the evaluator to distinguish among the various levels of performance on a continuum from poor to excellent. If the system is fair, easy to administer and so forth and it is not capable of allowing an evaluator to make this basic important distinction between acceptable and unacceptable performance, then the system should be modified or eliminated and a modified or new system developed.

SELECTED BIBLIOGRAPHY

1. *A Scheme for Evaluation and an Organizational Structure of Variables.* Tucson, Arizona: Educational Innovators Press, 1970

2. Biddle, Bruce J. and Ellena, William J., *Contemporary Research on Teacher Effectiveness.* New York: Holt, Rinehard and Winston, 1964.

3. Bloom, Benjamin S., *Taxonomy of Educational Objectives Handbook I: Cognitive Domain.* New York: David McKay Company, Inc., 1956.

4. Bradford, E. Doremus, A. & Kreismer, C., *Elementary School Evaluation: Administrator's Guide to Accountability,* Apr. '72, Parker.

5. Brighton, Staynor and Rose, Gale. *Increasing Your Accuracy in Teacher Evaluation.* Englewood Cliffs, N.J.: Prentice-Hall, Inc., 1965.

6. Callahan, M., *The Effective School Department Head,* '71, Parker.

7. *Case Studies.* Tucson, Arizona: Educational Innovators Press, 1970.

8. *Coding and Writing Test Items.* Tucson, Arizona: Educational Innovators Press, 1970.

9. Cornell, Terry D. *Educational Accountability: A Format for Monitoring the Teaching-Learning Process.* Tucson, Arizona: Educational Innovators Press, 1970.

10. *Developing and Writing Behavioral Objectives.* Tucson, Arizona: Educational Innovators Press, 1970.

11. *Evaluation Design.* Tucson, Arizona: Educational Innovators Press, 1970.

12. Flanagan, John C., Shanner, William M., and Mager, Robert F. *Language Arts Behavioral Objectives a Guide to Individualizing Learning.* Palo Alto, California: Westinghouse Learning Press, 1971.

13. Flanagan, John C., Shanner, William M., and Mager, Robert F. *Mathematics Behavioral Objectives a Guide to Individualizing Learning.* Palo Alto, California: Westinghouse Learning Press, 1971.

14. Flanagan, John C., Shanner, William M., and Mager, Robert F. *Science Behavioral Objectives a Guide to Individualizing Learning.* Palo Alto, California: Westinghouse Learning Press, 1971.

15. Flanagan, John C., Shanner, William M., and Mager, Robert F. *Social Studies Behavioral Objectives a Guide to Individualizing Learning.* Palo Alto, California: Westinghouse Learning Press, 1971.

16. Gage, N. L., *Handbook of Research on Teaching.* Chicago, Illinois: Rand McNally and Company, 1963.

17. Herman, W., *Principal's Guide to Teacher Personnel Problems in the Elementary Schools,'*66, Parker.

18. Johnson Stuart R. and Johnson, Rita B., *Developing Individualized Instructional Material.* Palo Alto, California: Westinghouse Learning Press, 1970.

19. Krathwohl, et. al., *Taxonomy of Educational Objectives Handbook II: Affective Domain.* New York: David McKay Company, Inc., 1964.

20. Mager, Robert F., *Preparing Instructional Objectives.* Palo Alto, California: Fearon Publisher, Inc., 1962.

21. *Needs Assessment.* Tucson, Arizona: Educational Innovators Press, 1970.

22. *Performance and Process Objectives.* Tuscon, Arizona: Educational Innovators Press, 1970.

23. *Proposal Guidelines.* Tuscon, Arizona: Educational Innovators Press, 1971.

24. Redfern, George B., *How to Appraise Teaching Performance.* Columbus, Ohio: School Management Institute, Inc., 1963.

25. Roberson, E. Wayne. *Developing Observation Systems.* Tucson, Arizona: Educational Innovators Press, 1970.

26. Rosenshine, Barak. "Evaluation of Classroom Instruction", *Review of Educational Research,* Volume 40, Number 2 (April, 1970), 279-300.

27. Simon, Anita and Boyer, Gil E., *Mirrors for Behavior an Anthology of Classroom Observation Instruments.* Philadelphia, Pennsylvania: Research for Better Schools, Inc., 1968.

28. Steig, L. R., & Frederick R. K., *School Personnel and In-Service Training Programs,* 1969, Parker.

29. *The Evaluatee Evaluates the Evaluator.* Circular No. 5, Washington, D. C.: Educational Research Service, American Association of School Administrators, 1970.

Six

ESTABLISHING THE GOALS AND PROCEDURES FOR A SYSTEM OF ADMINSTRATIVE EVALUATION

This chapter and Chapter 7 will present practical examples of types of activities that must be undertaken in developing a scheme of administrative evaluation. The major points of discussion will evolve around the: (1) Programming of goals, (2) Detailing the procedures, (3) Arriving at the techniques to be employed, (4) Deciding on the personnel to do the evaluations and (5) Planning a scheme which permits a means of evaluating the evaluators and the program of evaluation that has been established. Chapter 6 will present materials on the programming of goals and on detailing the procedures, and Chapter 7 will present materials on the remaining areas.

PROGRAMMING THE GOALS

The initial step in the development of a scheme for administrative evaluation is that of devoting a great deal of time with all individuals who are to be evaluated or who are to be responsible for conducting evaluations in dialoguing the goals to be achieved. From past experience certain basic assumptions, such as the following, will result from these initial discussions:

1. Administration is a valuable and necessary function in any school district.
2. Administration has, as its basic purpose, the improvement of the instructional environment of youngsters.
3. Administration is a supportive function. Administrators must monitor all systems, perform regulatory duties, evaluate staff and programs and they must facilitate sub-system goal achievement—all with the ultimate purpose of helping the total staff do a better job of educating youngsters.
4. Administration is a whole band of responsibility that must be performed by a team of individuals assigned to the administrative function. To best accomplish the administrative function, a team approach is necessary, and a clear division of labor which prevents undesirable overlap is imperative.
5. Each administrator has areas of strength and areas of weakness. Recognition of this fact allows each administrator to be less than a supreme being. It also allows the development of an individualized job upgrading program, and it permits other members of the administrative team to assist in filling the identifiable areas of weakness.
6. The staff needs to be formally evaluated, and administrators should be willing to subject themselves to evaluation.
7. Evaluation is necessary if planned change and improvement are to take place.
8. Although evaluation is difficult, administrators must be willing to try.
9. Evaluation is necessary, but it is very difficult to determine what to evaluate, who is to evaluate and how evaluation is to be done.

After many additional hours of discussion, goals such as the following will be determined. It should be remembered that even goals are subject to change over time.

Goal #1—To arrive at a division of labor which will permit a maximal administrative effort with a minimal amount of duplication of effort.

Goal #2—To allow the person being evaluated and the person doing the evaluation to realize the exact tasks and responsibilities assigned to each individual.

Goal #3—To permit the administrator and his immediate supervisor to establish mutually agreed upon yearly priorities to be accomplished.

Goal #4—To permit a face-to-face discussion of achievements and areas of weakness that need be improved.

This assumes that the immediate supervisor will also take the responsibility for assisting the administrator being evaluated in a program of improving the areas of weakness that have been identified.

Goal #5—To assist in tenure decisions.

Goal #6—To assist in determining salary for subsequent years.

Goal #7—To assist in building a record for future use in promotional decisions and in decisions of administrative assignment.

DETAILING THE PROCEDURES

One excellent means of detailing the procedures that need be arrived at in developing a total administrative evaluative scheme is to spell out the total administrative functions to be performed, to arrive at a decision as to which administrators are to perform which functions and to what degree, to establish a time and task schedule for completion of the procedural plan and to establish a methodology for the plan to become operational.

1. *Listing total administrative functions*—Although the finalized listing of administrative functions to be performed would be too detailed to include within this chapter, the stages of evolution can be demonstrated by the minutes of two of the weekly administrative meetings conducted by the Lewiston-Porter Central School District of Youngstown, New York (Figure 6-1 and 6-2).

2. *Arriving at who does what*—Once the total administrative functions are agreed upon, agreement needs to be reached as to which administrators are to perform which functions and to what degree they are to perform their functions. Obviously, the best way to arrive at this allotment of functions, is to have all administrators participate in the allotment of duties. If a comprehensive approach is taken to job descriptions, a written outline of decisions will be recorded for operational direction.

LEWISTON-PORTER CENTRAL SCHOOL
ADMINISTRATIVE INSTRUCTIONAL COUNCIL

Tuesday, August 26, 1969

SUGGESTED LIST OF ADMINISTRATIVE FUNCTIONS

1. Make recommendations to the Board of Education.

2. Execute Board of Education policy.

3. Report to the Board of Education on educational matters.

4. Assume responsibility for the educational plant, its care and maintenance.

5. Be involved in building construction.

6. Be responsible for school property and equipment.

7. Organize and supervise cafeterias.

8. Organize, coordinate and supervise the transportation of students.

9. Provide general education for all children in the district.

10. Recommend special education programs for handicapped pupils.

11. Recommend special services such as guidance, psychological and health services.

12. Develop appropriate marking and reporting systems.

13. Provide free textbooks and supplies used in instruction.

14. Maintain attendance accounting.

15. Decide upon matters of pupil discipline, suspension or exclusion.

16. Provide testing services.

17. Plan athletic and recreation programs.

18. Organize instructional media centers and audio-visual services.

19. Recruit, orient, supervise and make recommendations concerning staff personnel.

20. Provide educational leadership.

21. Encourage innovation and change.

22. Process grievances.

23. Participate in the negotiations process.

Figure 6-1

24. Make decisions concerning shared services (BOCES), state and federal programs.

25. Keep necessary reports and records.

26. Be active in planning, both for immediate needs and for the future.

27. Organize conferences and other in-service training programs.

28. Provide adequate evaluation of the total organization.

29. Be concerned with internal communication.

30. Keep handbooks and brochures current.

31. Assist with newsletters and other information releases.

32. Participate in planned public relations.

33. Encourage adult education.

34. Supervise community use of school facilities.

35. Cooperate with clergy in released time programs.

36. Recommend budget and supervise financial accounting.

37. Expedite coordination throughout the district.

Figure 6-1

LEWISTON-PORTER CENTRAL SCHOOL

Meeting Regarding Organizational Structure - October 28, 19

PERSONNEL

1. Assume responsibility to the Superintendent of Schools for all functions assigned.

2. Conduct of negotiations by the Administrative Assistant to the Superintendent of Schools.

3. Contract management interpretation by the Administrative Assistant to the Superintendent.

4. Process grievances.

5. Work with total administrative staff in the development of yearly and future personnel needs for all categories of employees (includes staffing standards and ratios.)

Figure 6-2

6. Coordinate recruitment schedules, brochures and cultivate source of
    supply.

7. Make recommendations for employment.

8. Coordinate the assignment of staff including substitute teachers,
    student teachers and teachers of co-curricular activities requiring
    extra pay.

    a) initial placement

    b) transfers

    c) reassignment

    d) retirement

    e) promotion

    f) tenure recommendations

    g) leaves of absence

9. Coordinate staff orientation - inservice.

10. Develop all personnel record systems and maintain all records except
    payroll records.

    a) health

    b) educational training and experience

    c) certification

    d) salary placement

    e) evaluation materials

    f) retirement

    g) leaves of absence

    h) applications

11. Assume responsibility to the Superintendent of Schools for mainten-
    ance of certificated, civil service and district employment standards.

12. Coordinate the development and maintenance of up-to-date job descrip-
    tions.

13. Conduct desirable research and production of desired yearly reports.

14. Develop and maintain statistics on (1) reasons for entry or exit,
    (2) pupil-teacher ratios, (3) etc.

15. Coordinate exit interviews.

16. Suggest to the Superintendent of Schools policies and regulations in the area of personnel services.

17. Develop and control budget for centralized personnel services.

18. Act as an advisor to the administrative staff in all areas of personnel services.

19. Conduct individual and group counseling sessions as deemed necessary to promote good personnel practices.

20. Evaluate personnel assigned to this function.

PUPIL PERSONNEL

1. Coordinate the guidance program. (Supervision of guidance personnel under building principal of building assigned.)

2. Coordinate the student record system.

3. Maintain records of attendance and health.

4. Maintain total records of resident students attending outside agencies.

5. Assume responsibility for health services and health service personnel.

6. Assume responsibility for psychological services and psychological service personnel.

7. Conduct and maintain the annual census.

8. Conduct research evaluation and produce desirable yearly reports.

9. Coordinate with outside agencies which offer additional pupil personnel services and coordinate and maintain a system of referral records to such agencies.

10. Develop and control budget for centralized pupil personnel services.

11. Act as an advisor to the instructional staff in areas of pupil personnel services.

12. Suggest to the Superintendent of Schools policies and rules and regulations relating to pupil personnel services.

13. Evaluate personnel assigned to this function.

Figure 6-2 (cont.)

Questions

1. Grievance - Who should handle?

2. One or two staff members?

3. Where does pupil personnel services go?

It was agreed that three (3) secretaries are needed:

1. Personnel coordinator,

2. Pupil personnel.

3. Psychological secretarial.

BUSINESS

Directly responsible to the Superintendent of Schools for:

1. Transportation services.

2. Cafeteria service.

3. Buildings and grounds service.

> NOTE: Responsible for the use of buildings for after school
> activities and on days when school is not in session.

4. Data processing services.

5. Budget control.

6. Payroll related services and records.

7. Accounting and auditing.

8. Purchasing.

9. Inventory control.

10. Central warehousing.

11. Fund management and investment.

12. Business function related records.

13. Research, evaluation and desirable yearly reports.

14. Consultation to the administrative staff in area of business.

15. Recommendations to the Superintendent of Schools policy changes,
    rules and regulations in the area of business.

16. Textbook distribution and control systems.

17. Control of fixed charges.

18. Control of activities related to Public Law 874.

19. Assisting in budget planning.

20. Evaluating personnel assigned to this function.

Important Divisions

     Business Manager

     Cafeteria Manager

     Superintendent of Buildings and Grounds

     Warehouse Manager

INSTRUCTION

Report directly to the Superintendent of Schools.

Assistant Superintendent for Instruction

Principal

Assistant Principal (Administrative responsibilities)	Assistant Principal (Instructional responsibilities)
a. Scheduling	a. Visit classes
b. Discipline	b. Evaluation
c. Pupil personnel services	c. Building in-service
d. Co-curricular	d. Curriculum development
	e. Act as sponsor for Student Council, Honor Society, and Senior Class.

Instruction

Speech & Hearing Specialist	Media Coordinator
Special Education Programming	Reading Coordinator
	Coordinator of Athletics & Phys. Ed.
	Continuing Education
	Summer School
	Math-Science Coordinator
	English-Social Studies Coordinator

It was agreed that funds ($10,000) for in-service and development of curriculum should be a budget item.

Figure 6-2 (cont.)

A discussion was held regarding curriculum development which resulted in
several different approaches:

1. Place Assistant Principals in all schools charged with the
   responsibility for curriculum development.

2. Assistant Principals in schools meeting standards for Assistant
   Principals charged with curriculum development.

3. Appoint a curriculum expert under instruction.

4. Use subject or combined subject area coordinators.

The next meeting will be held on November 4th at 9:00 a.m. at the
Balmer Road conference room.

Agenda:

   Each person to develop his own organization for the instructional
area.

3. *Developing a time and task completion schedule*—A two year
   schedule of development could well be similar to that listed
   below:

   Year one:

   July 7th—Discuss the positive and negative aspects of formalized administrative evaluation.

   July 16th—Decide as to whether an attempt at formalized
   evaluation is to be undertaken.

   July 23rd—Arriving at tasks to be performed.

   July 30th—Decide on which administrators are to do the leg
   work on each task.

   August and September—Complete sub-group and individualized
   work assignments.

   October 6th—Review of work to this point.

   October 13th—Review continued.

   October 20th—Discuss total administrative tasks to be performed.

   October 27th—Review of total administrative tasks to be performed.

November 3rd—Review continued.

November 10th—Make finalized decision on total administrative tasks.

November 11th—Discuss job descriptions to be written.

November 18th—Discuss job descriptions—continued.

November 25th—Agree on format for written job descriptions.

December 2nd—Assign to various administrators, the writing of initial drafts of specific job descriptions.

December, January and February—Work on initial write-ups of job descriptions.

March and April—Review specific job descriptions, rewrites, finalize each job description.

April 28th—Review all job descriptions and modifications of same to allow total coverage of all administrative functions.

May 9th—Print out and distribute all job descriptions.

May 12th—Discuss yearly performance objectives.

May 19th—Finalize format for yearly performance objectives.

May 26—Finalize write-up by each administrator and his immediate supervisor of individual performance objectives.

June 2nd—Discuss the dates for evaluations, and make decisions as to who shall do them.

June 9th—Decide on the format to be followed in conducting the evaluations.

June 16th—Decide on whether or not this should be tied to salary considerations.

June 23rd—Discuss whether or not implementation, on a trial basis should take place.

June 30th—Decide on whether feasibility pilot year is to be attempted.

Year two:

Evaluation of system, instruments and procedures; modifications as needed; decisions as to whether or not continuance is desirable and plan for future development and evaluation.

4. *Establishing a methodology to be followed*—Any methodology that is finally determined should be fitted to the local district's needs. An example of a finalized methodology which incorporated performance pay is that of the Godwin Heights Public Schools of Wyoming, Michigan (see Figure 6-3). Additional examples of instruments used in Godwin will be presented under the section of Chapter 7 dealing with techniques.

GODWIN HEIGHTS PUBLIC SCHOOLS
Wyoming, Michigan
ADMINISTRATIVE SALARY SCHEDULE
(Adopted for calendar year beginning July 1, 1969)

POSITION

Schedule Step	Salary Minimums	Salary Maximums
Administrative Assistant to the Superintendent (this is a training position)	$ 12,000	$ 15,000
Assistant Community Schools Director and Assistant Principals	$ 13,000	$ 16,000
Elementary Principals	$ 14,000	$ 19,000
Junior High or Middle School Principals	$ 14,500	$ 19,500
Community Schools Director Senior High Principal Director of Student Instructional Service Centers	$ 15,500	$ 21,250

Additions to Basic Schedule Above:

1. Educational Specialist or MA+30 = Add $750.00 to salary each year.

2. Doctorate = Add $1,000.00 to salary each year. (A person having both MA+30 and doctorate would have $1,750.00 added to salary each year.)

3. The Board will pay the complete costs of the MEA Insurance Package or an equivalent policy that has been approved by the Board up to $35.00 per month. This is to take place as soon as it is possible to allow enrollment in a plan.

Figure 6-3

Notations to Accompany Administrative Salary Schedule

1. This schedule is based on a 52-week contract with 20 work days of paid vacation per year included. Vacation shall be earned at the rate of two (2) days for each twenty (20) days worked up to a maximum of twenty (20) days per year. Vacation days can be accumulated to a maximum of fifty (50) days. If not used beyond fifty (50) days, the administrator loses these days **nor** does he receive pay for them.

2. Administrators are granted one (1) day of sick leave per twenty (20) work days, which are accrued after said twenty (20) days are worked.

3. Each administrator shall be assigned district-wide responsibility, other than his basic assignment, by the superintendent. Any principal who is assigned to a building of more than 500 students shall receive a $500.00 contract rider for each additional responsibility. In cases where the principal has assistants, the total number of students shall be divided by the number of administrators assigned in order to determine whether or not he qualifies for a contract rider.

4. A minimum standard of a master's degree, which includes at least 30 semester hours of graduate work, is established for all administrative positions. No additional compensation shall be granted for possession of a master's degree.

5. A newly-contracted administrator may be placed upon any step for the position contracted, based upon the superintendent's recommendation.

6. MERIT GROWTH STEPS - The Board of Education shall provide salary increases up through a maximum of three (3) merit growth steps beyond the current yearly salary, freeze the salary at the current level, or provide a salary decrease up through a maximum of one (1) year below the current

Figure 6-3 (cont.)

yearly salary. The only exception to merit increment increases is for an administrator who is new to Godwin and who has no previous administrative experience. In the case of inexperienced administrators they will be provided with an automatic $750.00 increment for each of the first two years of service. They will qualify for merit consideration after the initial two-year period.

The Board of Education shall base its salary determination upon a yearly evaluation of each administrator below the rank of assistant superintendent. Said yearly evaluations shall be conducted for each administrator by the central office administration. The assistant superintendents shall independently evaluate each administrator and submit their evaluations to the superintendent. The superintendent shall independently evaluate each administrator and he shall submit copies of all evaluations that have been conducted by the central office administration to each school board member; except that those positions of assistant principal and assistant community school director shall be evaluated by their immediate supervisor and the assistant superintendent for instruction. The Board of Education shall then establish the succeeding year's salary for each administrator.

The initial evaluation by the central office administration shall summarize all previous years of service by the administrator being evaluated. Subsequent evaluations shall be based only upon the past year of service.

7. Multiple year contracts, up through a maximum of three years, may be granted when recommended by the superintendent of schools and approved by the Board of Education. Multiple year contracts shall only state the first year's salary and shall incorporate the merit pay proposal that is operative.

Seven

DETAILING THE PROCEDURES
AND TECHNIQUES FOR A SYSTEM
OF ADMINSTRATIVE EVALUATION

This chapter picks up from Chapter 6, which discussed the areas of programming goals and detailing procedures. The major points to be covered in this chapter will concentrate on: (1) Arriving at the techniques to be employed, (2) Deciding on the personnel to do the evaluations and (3) Planning a scheme which permits a means of evaluating the evaluators and the program of evaluation that has been established.

ARRIVING AT TECHNIQUES TO BE EMPLOYED

The techniques to be utilized in administrative evaluations need vary with each district's purpose. However, observations, written evaluations, face-to-face conferences and periodic reviews are requisites to any workable system of administrative evaluation. Three concrete examples are presented dealing with the areas of job descriptions, performance objectives and forms to be utilized in written evaluative records.

1. *Job Descriptions*—Job descriptions can be comprehensive

130

statements of duties and responsibilities or they can merely list major functions to be performed. Examples of comprehensive job descriptions from the Lewiston-Porter Central School District of Youngstown, New York (Figures 7-1 and 7-2) indicate the team approach to junior high administration. These job descriptions also tie the junior high administration into the total district's administrative functions. The position examples are those of junior high principal, junior high assistant principal for instruction and junior high assistant principal for administration. The specific building involved has over 1,200 students.

2. *Performance Objectives*—Performance objectives should be established by mutual agreement between the administrator and his immediate supervisor. They should be done at least annually, and they should be relatively few in number. These yearly objectives should become the priority achievement goals to be accomplished by the individual administrator during the course of one year. They should be eliminated, carried over into the subsequent year and/or modified based upon the performance that has been exhibited over the course of the year just completed. An example of a list of performance objectives is that provided for the Superintendent of Buildings and Grounds of the Lewiston-Porter Central School District of Youngstown, New York for a recent year.

3. *Written Evaluation Forms*—The forms to be used in evaluation must vary with the individual school district's needs. Any form that is developed must be modified over a time period as needs continue to change. Examples of the forms utilized by the Godwin Heights Public Schools of Wyoming, Michigan, are presented in Figures 7-5 and 7-6. An instrument of self evaluation is presented to the principal being evaluated two weeks prior to his evaluation conference (Figure 2-1). Following the conference, a written narrative of strengths and weaknesses is given the administrator by the supervisor conducting the evaluation (Figure 7-5) also has space for brief narrative comments. Form III, (Figure 7-6), categorizes areas of narrative responses. Each of the three forms is utilized by a different evaluator, and

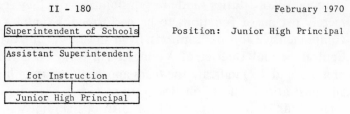

II - 180   February 1970

Superintendent of Schools   Position: Junior High Principal

Assistant Superintendent

for Instruction

Junior High Principal

I. Qualifications

    A. Required Qualifications

        1. Shall hold or be eligible for New York State's
            permanent certification qualifying him for this
            position.

        2. Shall possess five (5) years of educational experi-
            ence which shall include a minimum of three (3)
            years of administrative experience.

        3. Shall hold a Masters degree with studies in adminis-
            tration, supervision and curriculum.

    B. Desirable Qualifications

        1. Possesses a broad background of education experience
            in the areas of administration, supervision, teaching
            and curriculum development.

        2. Keeps himself informed about new developments in the
            educational areas of supervision, administration,
            research, philosophy, psychology, media, child develop-
            ment, curriculum and co-curricular activities. He
            also keeps informed about methodologies and new

Figure 7-1

developments in specific areas such as reading,

statistics, guidance, group dynamics and academic

areas.

3. Has the ability to work cooperatively with individuals

and groups of individuals in the solution of problems

and the implementation of innovative programs.

4. Has a knowledge of human relations and the ability

to communicate with staff and administration.

5. Has leadership abilities and skills to allow him to

organize and maintain successful workshops, instruc-

tional committees and other group activities.

6. Possesses a high degree of public presence and skill

in both personal and public relationships.

7. Has the ability to work democratically without relin-

quishing his leadership role.

II. Duties and Responsibilities

A. General Duties and Responsibilities

The Junior High Principal is directly responsible

to the Assistant Superintendent for Instruction

within the framework of the policies of the Board

of Education for the administration, supervision

and evaluation in matters pertaining to the manage-

ment of the Junior High School. He is responsible

for the organization, coordination, supervision,

evaluation and interpretation of the total instructional program in the Junior High School. Further, he is responsible for the overall safety and welfare of the entire personnel and is also responsible for all public and parent information programs and is the initial contact for the public and parents.

B. Specific Duties and Responsibilities

1. Develops the program of studies consistent with the needs of students and State mandates and works with the Assistant Superintendent for Instruction in the development of curriculum.

2. Organizes and supervises the faculty with responsibility for the balanced assignment of curricular and co-curricular duties.

3. Assists in the inauguration of carefully designed experimentation and in the evaluation of said experimentation.

4. Visits classrooms and occasionally performs as a substitute teacher in order to maintain a knowledge of on-line procedures and problems.

5. Supervises and implements the development of the master schedule of classes and individual student schedules.

6. Completes and forwards to the Assistant Superintendent for Instruction an annual written performance evaluation of all personnel assigned to his charge.

7. Makes recommendations to the Assistant Superintendent

Figure 7-1 (cont.)

for Instruction regarding leaves of absence, suspensions, dismissals, probationary status and tenure status of all teachers, assistant principals and other personnel for whom he holds responsibility.

8. Recommends to the Assistant Superintendent for Instruction all additions, deletions and modifications in instructional programs and courses of study.

9. Is responsible for the supervision of his probationary and tenure teachers and prepares written supervisory reports.

10. Assists in the development of in-service education programs for the professional staff.

11. Is responsible for the development and operation of administrative systems in his building and supervises the work of non-certified employees and makes evaluation reports as required for supervisory and salary increment purposes.

12. Submits an annual progress report to the Assistant Superintendent for Instruction in June of each year. Such report shall include an assessment of the past year's activities, and of the future objectives for improvement of the instructional program for the succeeding year together with a five (5) year projection of needs in the area of instruction.

13. Surveys staff needs and makes recommendations to the Assistant Superintendent for Instruction.

14. Works with the Director of Personnel Services in the

recruitment and interviewing of teachers and makes
recommendations to the Assistant Superintendent for
Instruction concerning the initial employment of
teachers and staff members.

15. Assists the Assistant Superintendent for Instruction
and the Director of Personnel Services in the planning and implementation of the orientation program
for new members of the staff.

16. Works cooperatively with other administrators, staff,
students and community groups.

17. Provides for increasing individualization of instruction for his students and assignment differentiation
for his staff.

18. Works cooperatively with the school business office
in arranging procedures for accounting operations
pertaining to the Junior High School.

19. Works cooperatively with the building administrative
and teaching staff in the selection of textbooks,
equipment and teaching materials, and makes recommendations for the purchase of the same to the Assistant
Superintendent for Instruction.

20. Is responsible for the proper administration and
supervision of all testing and examinations, and for
the preparation and submission of reports to the
Assistant Superintendent for Instruction and the
State Education Department.

21. Organizes and supervises guidance and counseling
services for his building.

22. Organizes a system for reporting to parents, recording such reports and maintaining with the guidance
department, follow-up procedures.

Figure 7-1 (cont.)

23. Reviews psychological referrals, and with the cooperation of the guidance department, provides follow-up procedures for students within the building.

24. Determines students' assignments.

25. Establishes and checks regularly the eligibility of students for participation in activities.

26. Organizes and supervises a system of attendance, discipline, activities and welfare for all students.

27. Supervises Junior High School activities sponsored by the school and held in his building.

28. Coordinates with the appropriate building principal the supervision of all school sponsored activities originating in another building and held in the Junior High School.

29. Organizes, coordinates and implements all student activities and exercises control of activity funds in accordance with approved accounting procedures.

30. Cooperates with the Director of Athletics and Intramurals in the assignment of school personnel involved in athletics or intramurals in his building.

31. Organizes and conducts regular meetings with the school psychologist, nurse, guidance department and assistant principals to discuss student problems.

32. Develops information on needs for home instruction and submits requests to the Assistant Superintendent for Instruction. He also maintains the attendance of pupils in his building on home instruction and prepares the payroll for personnel instructing the students of his building.

33. Is responsible for administration of free lunch programs.

34. Prepares a calendar of school programs and activities for coordination with the needs of other buildings and areas and also district plans.

35. Develops and submits budget requests to the Assistant Superintendent for Instruction for all junior high school programs.

36. Administers the approved building budget by seeing that expenditures are within the approved budgetary allotments.

37. Prepares the payroll for the staff of the building and submits it to the Business Manager.

38. Reports annually recommendations on building maintenance and repairs to the Superintendent of Buildings and Grounds.

39. Is responsible for the inventory of all the building textbooks and equipment for the instructional program.

40. Has the responsibility for the preparation and review of building use requests for all school activities under his direction and submits building use requests to the appropriate authorities.

41. Organizes and supervises fire, civil defense and bus drills and reports same to the proper authorities.

42. Schedules faculty meetings as the need arises.

43. Obtains all professional materials from the State Education Department as they become available for all teachers in his building.

44. Is responsible for checking all end-of-year obligations of faculty and students.

45. Meets with building representatives for the purpose of reviewing problems that may affect the faculty.

Figure 7-1 (cont.)

46. Is responsible for hearing the first level of the grievance procedure from members of the junior high staff.

47. Assists appropriate personnel in development of handbooks for teachers, substitute teachers, student teachers and students.

48. Keeps informed regarding the changing role of the Junior High Principal through attendance at administrative meetings and conferences and continued professional study.

49. Attends all meetings of the Board of Education, the Administrative Instructional Council and the Superintendent's Instructional Council.

50. Assists in the development of educational specifications for new buildings when so directed by the Assistant Superintendent for Instruction.

51. Assists the Board of Education, the Superintendent of Schools, and the Assistant Superintendent for Instruction with the interpretation of the instructional program to the community and he serves as the agent of communications between the Assistant Superintendent for Instruction's office and the Board of Education, the community and the staff when so directed by the Assistant Superintendent for Instruction.

52. Develops and maintains a positive communications system with the community, teaching staff, administrators and the Board of Education. This implies the continuous maintenance of an open door policy so that all staff members feel welcome to discuss policies or problems.

II - 190   March 19

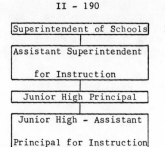

Position: Junior High - Assistant

Principal for Instruction

I. Qualifications

   A. Required Qualifications

      1. Shall hold or be eligible for New York State's permanent certification qualifying him for this position.

      2. Shall possess five (5) years of educational experience.

      3. Shall hold a Masters degree with studies in administration, supervision and curriculum.

   B. Desirable Qualifications

      1. Possesses broad experience in education including teaching, administration and supervision.

      2. Has a knowledge of the principles and the research underlying curriculum development.

      3. Works cooperatively with individuals and groups of individuals in the solution of problems and the implementation of innovative programs.

      4. Possesses a knowledge of human relations and has the ability to communicate with staff and administration.

      5. Has an understanding of the varied approaches in the teaching-learning process.

      6. Has a knowledge of theories of learning, child development and group processes and possesses the ability to communicate with staff and administration on these matters.

Figure 7-2

7.   Possesses the ability to become increasingly knowledgeable and to grow in sensitivity and skill as a
leader in curriculum development.

8.   Possesses a high degree of public presence and skill
in both personal and public relationships.

9.   Has the ability to work democratically without relin-
quishing his leadership role.

II.   Duties and Responsibilities

A.   General Duties and Responsibilities

The Junior High Assistant Principal for Instruction
is directly responsible to the Junior High Principal
for the supervision, coordination, implementation
and evaluation of matters pertaining to instruction
within the Junior High School.

B.   Specific Duties and Responsibilities

1.   Acts as principal of the school in the absence of
the principal and the Assistant Principal for Administration.

2.   Acts as sponsor for student council and honor society.

3.   Administers and supervises students participating in
television, radio and related curricular activities
in cooperation with other appropriate personnel.

4.   Is responsible for student teacher assignments and
visitation of college supervisors within the building.

5.   Approves national, state or local contest participation for the building.

6.   Assists teachers in the development of teaching units
and in the evaluation of students in behavioral terms.

7.   Assists the principal and teachers in selection of
instructional aids.

8. Assists the staff in adapting to learning theories
   and curriculum innovations.

9. Visits classrooms and occasionally performs as a
   substitute teacher in order to maintain a knowledge
   of on-line procedures and problems.

10. Serves as a member of the Superintendent's Instruc-
    tional Council and attends all meetings of the Admin-
    istrative Instructional Council.

11. Makes suggestions to the building principal as to
    building staff in-service needs relating to instruc-
    tion.

12. Assists in maintaining in-building professional and
    curricular materials libraries.

13. Plans, administers, and supervises parent night pro-
    grams related to guidance and counseling activities.

14. Assists the building principal in:

    a. planning and implementing curricular and co-curri-
       cular improvement within the building through
       committee work, experimentation and study groups.

    b. arranging professional faculty meetings relating
       to instruction.

    c. supervision and evaluation of probationary and
       tenure teachers and the preparation of supervisory
       reports. He also conducts supervisory conferences
       following supervisory visits.

    d. administering the special educational services
       within the building including SLD classes,
       educable classes, advanced placement classes,
       home study and students attending BOCES classes.

Figure 7-2 (cont.)

e.   preparation of budget requests for all instructional and curricular materials.

f.   helping teachers to introduce innovative methodology in their teaching.

g.   administering, supervising and evaluating the
instructional program.

h.   development of public relations programs.

i.   evaluating the guidance counseling services.

j.   placement of students, being responsible for
maintaining proper student-teacher ratios and
placement of students according to individual
needs.

k.   planning and implementing orientation programs
for new and substitute teachers relating to
instruction.

15.   Assists the building principal and the building
guidance department in:

a.   drop out studies.

b.   analysis of test results.

c.   follow-up studies.

d.   research reports on retention of students and
failure rates and patterns.

e.   identifying needs for course additions, deletions
and modifications.

f.   group and individual conferences as relates to
to student placement and instructional programming of students.

g.   remediation programs and enrichment programs
needed.

16. Submits an annual progress report to the building principal in June of each year. Such report shall include an assessment of the past year's activities, and of the future objectives for improvement of the instructional program for the succeeding year together with a five (5) year projection of needs in the area of instruction.

17. Develops and maintains a positive communications system with the community, teaching staff, administrators and the Board of Education. This implies the continuous maintenance of an open door policy so that all staff members feel welcome to discuss policies or problems in his area of responsibility.

18. Operates, and sees that his subordinates operate, within the letter and intent of legal mandates, Board of Education's policies and the Superintendent's rules and regulations.

19. Performs such other duties related to the instructional program as may be assigned by the building principal.

20. Performs in all instances as a subordinate officer of the building principal with integrity; honoring the confidences and loyalties ascribed to and required of this administrative position.

III. <u>Working Conditions</u>

Shall be in accordance with the working agreement negotiated by the Board of Education and the Lewiston-Porter Organization of Educational Administrators.

Figure 7-2 (cont.)

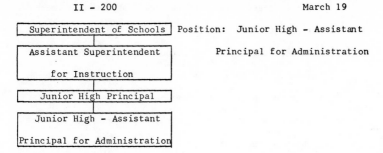

II - 200   March 19

| Superintendent of Schools | Position: Junior High - Assistant

| Assistant Superintendent   Principal for Administration

| for Instruction

| Junior High Principal |

| Junior High - Assistant
| Principal for Administration |

I. Qualifications

    A. Required Qualifications

        1. Shall hold or be eligible for New York State's permanent certification qualifying him for this position.

        2. Shall possess five (5) years of educational experience.

        3. Shall hold a Masters degree with studies in administration, supervision and curriculum.

    B. Desirable Qualifications

        1. Possesses broad experience in education including teaching, administration and supervision.

        2. Has a knowledge of the principles and the research underlying school administration.

        3. Works cooperatively with individuals and groups of individuals in the solution of problems.

        4. Possesses a knowledge of human relations and has the ability to communicate with staff and administration.

        5. Has an understanding of the curricular and co-curricular programs and has special interest in school management.

        6. Has a knowledge of theories of learning, child development and group processes and possesses the ability

Figure 7-3

to communicate with staff and administration on these
matters.

7. Possesses the ability to become increasingly knowledgeable and to grow in sensitivity and skill as a
   leader in school administration.

8. Possesses a high degree of public presence and skill
   in both personal and public relationships.

9. Has the ability to work democratically without relin-
   quishing his leadership role.

II. Duties and Responsibilities

A. General Duties and Responsibilities

The Junior High Assistant Principal for Administration
is directly responsible to the Junior High Principal
for the supervision, coordination, implementation
and evaluation of matters pertaining to the administration of the Junior High School.

B. Specific Duties and Responsibilities

1. Acts as principal of the school in the absence of
   the principal.

2. Plans and implements all administrative calendars
   for the building to which assigned.

3. Acts as the building coordinator of all co-curricular
   activities.

4. Administers and supervises student assembly programs,
   dramatic productions, pep rallies and speech and
   music productions.

5. Inspects the building and grounds and makes recommendations on building maintenance and repairs to the
   building principal.

Figure 7-3 (cont.)

6. Coordinates fire, civil defense and bus drills for his building.

7. Is responsible for administration and supervision of the cafeteria and school store.

8. Handles all student and staff fund drives within the building.

9. Coordinates community-school activities with the school activity program within the building.

10. Visits classrooms and occasionally performs as a substitute teacher in order to maintain a knowledge of on-line procedures and problems.

11. Attends all meetings of the Administrative Instructional Council.

12. Administers and supervises the attendance procedures, health and medical services for students in the building to which he is assigned.

13. Makes suggestions to the building principal as to building staff in-service needs relating to administration.

14. Reviews, recommends and processes all matters relating to textbooks, equipment and supplies.

15. Supervises student and staff attendance, maintaining up-to-date records, developing attendance procedures and notifying parents, juvenile authorities and/or police concerning violations.

16. Assists the building principal in:

    a. administering the counseling and guidance services and directly supervises master student scheduling.

    b. preparation of building requests relating to the administration of the building.

c. administering and supervising attendance, discipline and other activities relating to the welfare
of students in the building.

d. checking of end of year teacher responsibilities.

e. development of public relations programs.

f. planning and implementing orientation programs
for new and substitute teachers relating to
administration.

g. arranging professional faculty meetings relating
to administration.

17. Assists the principal and the building guidance
department in:

a. master class schedules.

b. attendance reporting and contact because of individual student's attendance irregularities.

c. the mechanics of administering and scoring
standardized and other tests.

d. student eligibility for athletics and other
co-curricular activities.

e. coordination of pupil records systems.

18. Submits an annual progress report to the building
principal in June of each year. Such report shall
include an assessment of the past year's activities,
and of the future objectives for improvement of the
administrative program for the succeeding year
together with a five (5) year projection of needs
in the area of instruction.

19. Develops and maintains a positive communications
system with the community, teaching staff, administrators and the Board of Education. This implies

Figure 7-3 (cont.)

the continuous maintenance of an open door policy
so that all staff members feel welcome to discuss
policies or problems in his area of responsibility.

20. Operates, and sees that his subordinates operate,
within the letter and intent of legal mandates,
Board of Education's policies and the Superintendent's
rules and regulations.

21. Performs such other duties related to the administrative program as may be assigned by the building
principal.

22. Performs in all instances as a subordinate officer
of the building principal with integrity; honoring
the confidences and loyalties ascribed to and required
of this administrative position.

III. Working Conditions

Shall be in accordance with the working agreement
negotiated by the Board of Education and the
Lewiston-Porter Organization of Educational Administrators.

LEWISTON-PORTER CENTRAL SCHOOL

PERFORMANCE OBJECTIVES: July 1, 1970 - June 30, 1971

Position: SUPERINTENDENT OF BUILDINGS AND GROUNDS

1. To work cooperatively with the Shift Supervisor in establishing his performance objectives for July 1, 1970-June 30, 1971.
These statements should be committed to writing and a copy
forwarded to the Superintendent of Schools. These statements,

Figure 7-4

along with his job description, will serve as basic tools for the yearly performance evaluations.

2. To develop a written 5 year preventative maintenance schedule and submit a copy to the Superintendent of Schools.

3. To develop a written 5 year paint schedule and submit a copy to the Superintendent of Schools.

4. To successfully utilize your Shift Supervisor.

5. To tag and inventory all equipment in the District. Such inventory should be done by building location, and should include the type of item, the tag serial number, the condition of the item and other pertinent information. All new items should be tagged before delivery and placed on the inventory; all items destroyed should be eliminated from the inventory. Said inventory is to be kept in written form, and should be accessible to the Superintendent of Schools and other administrators.

6. To submit, monthly, to the Superintendent of Schools, a written report of the condition of all buildings. Said report to be made after a physical visitation has been made by you.

7. To develop a written list of vacation and summer tasks to be performed by your personnel.

8. To perform to the best of your ability, all duties and responsibilities as listed in your job description.

Figure 7-4 (cont.)

GODWIN HEIGHTS PUBLIC SCHOOLS

Wyoming, Michigan

FORM II

Name of Principal_____

	1	2	3	4	5	6	7	8	9	10	N*
1. Parent Relations	Low									High	
2. Staff Relations											
3. Pupil Relations											
4. Planning and Executing In-Service Programs for Staff											
5. Curriculum Know How and Contributions											
6. Creative and Innovative in New Methods and Materials											
7. Delegation of Work to Right People											
8. Building - Environment											

Figure 7-5

	1	2	3	4	5	6	7	8	9	10	N*
9. Evaluation of Pupils and Teachers in Unobjective Manner	Low									High	
10. Communications											
11. Personality Factors											
12. Personal Appearance Factors											
13. Administration Relations											
14. Other											

*Not observed

Figure 7-5 (cont.)

GODWIN HEIGHTS PUBLIC SCHOOLS

Wyoming, Michigan

FORM III

Principal Evaluation Narrative

As an instructional leader:

    Comments: 1.

                2.

                etc.

Figure 7-6

As a pupil control agent or disciplinarian:

    Comments: 1.

                2.

                etc.

As a diplomat and/or mediator of various forces in the community such as P.T.A., etc.:

    Comments: 1.

                2.

                etc.

As a chief of non-teaching employees:

    Comments: 1.

                2.

                etc.

As an office manager and businessman who keeps track of budgets:

    Comments: 1.

                2.

                etc.

As a guidance person:

    Comments: 1.

                2.

                etc.

As an Innovator:

    Comments: 1.

                2.

                etc.

154 Detailing the Procedures and Techniques for Administrative Evaluation

all three are combined to arrive at a final face-to-face evaluative conference. Obviously, if a check list instrument is to be used, the items should be weighted in terms of their value to overall administrative performance.

It must always be remembered that one of the prime purposes of any evaluation, regardless of forms or methods used, is to assess job performance. Genuine compliments should be provided the individual in his areas of strength, and the identifiable areas of weakness should lead to an individualized in-service and job upgrading program geared to the specific needs of the individual administrator being evaluated. The burden of assistance lies squarely upon the shoulders of the supervisor who is conducting the evaluation.

DECIDING ON THE PERSONNEL TO DO THE EVALUATIONS

The persons who are to do the evaluations must be determined on the basis of the most reasonable decision for each local district, and a district need not limit its procedure to "one" method. In all cases, however, the minimal procedure should include a self-evaluation by an administrator and an evaluation by the administrator's immediate supervisor.

Multiple involvement acts as a check-and-balance system, and this procedure more quickly identifies the biases which may be consciously or subconsciously present. Finally, very serious consideration should be given to the possibility of teachers, classified staff, peers and students becoming involved in the evaluation of administrators occupying certain positions.

For example, let us take the hypothetical case of an elementary principal. He could develop, with his immediate supervisor, his job description and his yearly list of performance objectives. Some time later he could perform a self evaluation based upon these guidelines. He could also switch schools with another district elementary principal for one week, and the two elementary principals could then assist each other in evaluating their performances. He could ask the staff to use a commercial rating scale or develop a list of guidemarks that they consider important for a good principal to possess. He could then ask his teachers and other staff members, if he so desired, to rate him on the benchmarks that they have developed. Finally, he could ask his immediate supervisor to perform a series of interim evaluations prior to the formal yearly evaluative session.

PLANNING TO EVALUATE THE EVALUATORS
AND THE SYSTEM OF EVALUATION

Evaluators can be evaluated by means of assessing their consistency over a time period, and by measuring their evaluations of a specific individual or a group of individuals against the evaluations submitted by others evaluating the same individuals. If, in the process, an evaluator is found to be consistently high or low in his evaluations compared to the district's norm, a corrective formula can be devised to correct his uniform tendencies for over-estimation or under-estimation as compared to the norm. Finally, an evaluator who displays inconsistency in his evaluations over a period of time can either be trained, by an individualized in-service program, to become consistent, or he can be eliminated from the team that is held responsible for conducting the evaluations.

The best means of identifying the quality of the system of evaluation is by determining whether or not it works operationally. Certainly, modifications need be made in any evaluative scheme over a period of time. Over time needs change and skills needed to operate an effective school change. Some good examples of this are provided by the changes needed in administrative operations and administrative skills as the Nation's schools were introduced to large grants for those who could write and operate Federal programs, as the school districts adjusted, and continue to adjust, to a different form of governance brought about by the adoption of laws on collective bargaining in the public domain and as the districts adjusted to the influx of "new" curriculum programs as exemplified by SMSG Math, BSCS Biology and many others.

Getting back to the problem of whether or not the system of evaluation used is working, it appears that there are two prime methods of arriving at a determination on this matter. The initial check on whether or not the system is working can be made by allowing the individuals who have been evaluated and the individuals who have conducted the evaluations to tell those in decision making places whether or not they feel the system is fair, mechanically easy to administer, assists in identifying an individual's strengths and weaknesses and permits the development of more effective administration through job upgrading and improved administrative performance. The second check on whether or not the system works is one of determining whether or not it allows the evaluator to distinguish between excellent and poor overall performance. If the system is fair, easy to administer and so forth and it is not capable of allowing an evaluator to make this basic distinction between acceptable and unacceptable performance, then the system should be junked and a new system developed.

Eight

EVALUATING CLASSIFIED (NON-CERTIFIED) STAFF

The evaluative scheme for classified personnel roughly parallels the steps involved in the scheme applied to other employee groups. The crucial steps are: (1) programming the goals, (2) detailing the procedures, (3) arriving at the techniques to be employed during the evaluation process, (4) deciding on the personnel to do the evaluations, and (5) planning to evaluate the evaluators and the evaluation program that has been established. In addition, the techniques of quality control, cost efficiency analysis, cost effectiveness analysis, time allocations, error margins and work standards are quite readily applied to the work of many of the classified personnel operations. This chapter will limit its examples to the category of custodial services.

PROGRAMMING THE GOALS

Initially, much time must be spent by the individuals who are held responsible for the development of the evaluation system for classified personnel in discussion, and from past experiences, some basic assumptions, such as the following will evolve:

1. Classified personnel services are valuable and necessary to the smooth functional operation of any school district.
2. Classified personnel services has, as its basic purpose, the improvement of the learning environment for children. If this purpose is not served, there is no need for classified personnel services.
3. Classified personnel services perform supportive functions. For example:
   (a) custodial personnel are responsible for seeing that the school plant in which teachers teach and students learn, is kept well cleaned and well maintained.
   (b) secretarial personnel are responsible for the accurate and rapid reproduction and filing of student, teacher and administrator produced instructional materials and correspondence which are necessary to the efficient operation of the school district, and
   (c) food service personnel are responsible for seeing that students are fed a nutritious meal in a friendly atmosphere in order that the students are physically comfortable and relaxed for the afternoon study period.
4. Classified personnel services perform a large band of activities that must be performed by a team of individuals who are assigned these functions. In order to most effectively and efficiently conduct these tasks, a team approach is a necessity, and a clear division of labor is imperative.
5. Each classified employee has areas of strengths and areas of weakness. Recognition of this fact, while developing the evaluation plan, permits the development of meaningful individual and group job upgrading programs to be developed for the purpose of correcting the areas of weakness.
6. Each employee needs be evaluated in order that he improves his performance and in order that the school district benefit from the best services possible within the existing constraints.

Following many additional discussions, a listing of goals will evolve. However, it must be kept in mind that goals need be subject to change as the environmental variables change over time periods. No goal should be considered an absolute that is not subjective to review, modification and/or elimination.

Goal #1—To arrive at a division of labor that will permit the total classified staff to produce a maximum effort with a minimum amount of duplication.

Goal #2—To allow the person being evaluated and the person doing the evaluation to realize the specific tasks and responsibilities assigned to each individual.

Goal #3—To permit the employee and his immediate supervisor to establish performance goals that are to be accomplished over a definite time period.

Goal #4—To provide for genuine face-to-face discussion of achievements and areas of weakness that are in need of improvement. This provision assumes that the immediate supervisor will assist the employee being evaluated in a program designed to improve the areas of weakness that were identified.

Goal #5—To assist in the making of permanent appointments, under Civil Service, salary determinations, job assignments and promotional decision.

DETAILING THE PROCEDURES

Using the example category of cleaner, the procedures that would prove helpful are: (1) Establishing standards that are considered acceptable "average" outputs. These standards are both qualitive and quantitive in nature, (2) Arriving at an overview job description, and (3) Arriving at a list of tasks to be completed on a regularized daily, weekly, monthly, and yearly basis.

1. Establishing Standards

Standards may be set by various methods such as trial and error, by utilizing those that are reported in professional publications or by observation of what the "average" employee can do in a given period of time. Lewiston-Porter Central School of Youngstown, New York, established the standard of one cleaner for every 15,000 square feet with the following variables applied: (a) Add 1,000 square feet if the area is carpeted, (b) Subtract 100 square feet per each 1,000 square assigned for a building that is over 20 years old, and (c) Subtract 100 square feet per 1,000 square feet assigned for the areas in use at least 50% of the time in evenings and weekends.

Another method is to time each operation and total the amount that can be accomplished in an eight hour day. For example, it may take 8½ minutes to clean a water closet, it may take 17 minutes to dry mop a 900 square foot classroom; and many other similar tasks could be allocated a performance time.

A multiple factored formula approach can be demonstrated by that adopted by Godwin Heights Public School of Wyoming, Michigan. Godwin's formula is shown in Figure 8-1.

2. Arriving at an Overview Job Description

After determining the staffing standards, a listing of duties that are common to that job classification need be determined. The job description arrived at in the Lewiston—Porter System for the category of cleaner-maintenance helper is shown in Figure 8-2.

3. Arriving at Specific Daily, Weekly, Monthly and Yearly Tasks To Be Performed

The final step in determining the detailed procedures is to present each employee with a list of his regularized tasks. An example schedule is shown in Figure 8-3.

ARRIVING AT THE TECHNIQUES FOR EVALUATION

Dependent upon the specific position being evaluated, techniques may vary. A secretary might well be evaluated upon her ability to type a certain number of words per minute with an acceptable number of errors, her accuracy in filing and retrieving information, her ability to take raw data information and establish an acceptable report format, and other specific variables that can be measured. A food service helper may well be evaluated on the number of meals that she can produce, of an acceptable quality, per hour, the number of students she can serve per hour, and other specific task standards. For purposes of this discussion, however, let's return to the example of cleaner-maintenance helper.

By direct observation, almost anyone could determine whether wastebaskets have been emptied, windows have been cleaned, a carpet vacuumed and so forth. The adequacy of the standard of cleanliness has been established by the daily, weekly, monthly and yearly task assignment. If there is doubt about the adequacy of the standard, the administrator in charge should

1. One custodian for 8 teachers (only contractual classroom teachers). Any professional employee who is not a classroom teacher shall be counted at 1/10th of a classroom teacher.

$$\frac{\text{No. of teachers}}{8} = \text{Teacher Factor} \quad \text{(to 2 decimal points)}$$

2. One custodian for each 225 pupils.

$$\frac{\text{No. of pupils}}{225} = \text{Student Factor}$$

3. One custodian for every 11 rooms (this includes specialized rooms as one room, regardless of size -- it excludes storage, lavatory and small office rooms).

$$\frac{\text{No. of rooms}}{11} = \text{Room Factor}$$

4. One custodian for every 15,000 square feet of building area.

   (a) Besides actual square footage, add 100 square feet per 1,000 actual square footage for buildings over 20 years of age.

   (b) Besides actual square footage, add 100 square feet per 1,000 actual square footage for a building that has 5,000 or more square feet in use at least 3 days per week over normal school hours.

$$\frac{\text{Square feet}}{15,000} = \text{Square Footage Factor}$$

Figure 8-1

IV - 170   March 19

| Superintendent of Schools |
| Superintendent of Buildings and Grounds |
| Cleaner-Maintenance Helper |

Position: Cleaner-Maintenance
Helper

I. Qualifications (Reference: Niagara County Civil Service Specifications)

   A. Graduation from elementary school and any combination of experience and training sufficient to indicate the ability to do the work.

   B. Knowledge of building cleaning methods, procedures and equipment; ability to perform semi-skilled manual tasks without constant supervision; ability to understand and follow simple oral and written directions; willingness to perform routine cleaning and other manual tasks; ability to get along well with others; thoroughness; dependability and good physical condition.

Figure 8-2

II. <u>Duties and Responsibilities</u> (Reference: Niagara County Civil Service
Specifications)

A. <u>General Duties and Responsibilities</u>

Performs routine building cleaning work, semi-skilled manual
tasks and related work as required. These tasks involve the
thorough execution of cleaning tasks following a well established
routine, or the performing of painting and other semi-skilled
tasks under direct supervision.

B. <u>Specific Duties and Responsibilities</u> (Illustrative only)

1. Assists in painting and other semi-skilled tasks.

2. Mops and sweeps floors, stairs and hallways.

3. Dusts desks, woodwork, furniture and equipment.

4. Collects and disposes of trash and garbage and empties
waste baskets.

5. Delivers mail, packages and supplies.

6. Washes chalkboards, sinks and other fixtures.

7. Washes drapes and curtains and cleans venetian blinds.

8. Performs other duties as directed by the immediate
administrative supervisor.

9. Maintains the confidences required and serves with
loyalty and integrity to the Lewiston-Porter School
District and to the administrator assigned.

III. <u>Working Conditions</u> - As prescribed in the applicable negotiated
master agreement.

<u>NOTE</u>:   The administrator to whom the employee is assigned shall
submit a detailed job description, using the format above,
to the Director of Personnel Services and the Superintendent
of Schools in October of 1970. He shall list the name of
the employee and all specifics. He shall file an additional job description at any time that a modification takes
place in the tasks assigned or when a new individual fills
the position. Finally, any official report presented to
the Niagara County Civil Service Commission shall coincide,
exactly, with the above job description; and it shall be
reviewed with the Director of Personnel Services prior to
signature and submission to the Civil Service.

Figure 8-2 (cont.)

LEWISTON-PORTER CENTRAL SCHOOL
Youngstown, New York

Example Schedule for Cleaner-Maintenance Helper

_____   _____
Name of Employee   Building Assigned

You are an important member of the total employee group. It is your responsibility to provide a pleasant, clean and healthful environment in
which students learn. You are, therefore a very important person. Your
cleaning schedule consists of 16,000 square feet of carpeted area. You
are assigned rooms 117 through 133 including the adjoining corridor areas.
Your routine is as follows:

	Daily	Weekly	Monthly	Yearly
1. Vacuum area	x			
2. Dust rooms	x			
3. Clean glass		x		
4. Clean lavatories	x			
5. Clean chalkboards	x			
6. Check doors and windows to see that they are locked	x			
7. Empty wastebaskets	x			
8. Check heat and air conditioning controls in your area and reset as necessary		x		
9. Change burned out lights		x		
10. Clean venetian blinds			x	
11. Move out all furniture and condition clean carpeting				x (2 per yr.)
12. Paint areas indicated by your shift supervisor				x
13. Repair minor furniture and equipment damage				

Figure 8-3

	Daily	Weekly	Monthly	Yearly
14. Clean woodwork			x	
15. Perform special tasks requested by teachers in your assigned area	x			
16. Perform special tasks requested by principal in your assigned area	x			
17. Perform specialized tasks requested by your shift supervisor	x			
18. Et cetera				
19. Et cetera				

It would also be possible to assign a time factor to each task and arrive at a daily schedule similar to the following:

3:30 - 4:50 p.m.	clean 16 classroom lavatories (5 minutes each)
4:51 - 7:30 p.m.	vacuum, dust and clean chalkboards (8 rooms - 20 minutes each)
7:31 - 8:00 p.m.	lunch
8:01 - 10:40	vacuum, dust and clean chalkboards (8 rooms - 20 minutes each)
10:41 - 11:20	check controls, empty baskets, change lights
11:21 - 12:00	do specified tasks requested, or if none are requested, take a coffee break

Figure 8-3 (cont.)

temporarily assign one of his "average" workers to the area in question to see if the assigned tasks can be performed up to the acceptable standard of quality within the time allotted. If this can be done, the employee regularly assigned that area may need some in-service help to so perform, or, after a reasonable length of time, he may need be laid off. If the "average" cleaner cannot perform the tasks satisfactorily in the time assigned, the standards for the area should be modified.

DECIDING ON PERSONNEL TO PERFORM EVALUATIONS

The basic person who should be assigned the responsibility of evaluation is the employee's immediate supervisor. In the case of a cleaner-maintenance helper, this is the shift supervisor. There should be a periodically scheduled evaluation that should be committed to writing, and a conference should be held with the employee and a copy of the written evaluation given him. Further, if the employee disagrees with the evaluation, another administrator should be permitted to reevaluate the employee's work. In the case of the cleaner, this could be the Superintendent of Buildings and Grounds.

A form which allows for evaluation of general characteristics and for specific tasks judgement is most useful. A form similar to Figure 8-4 is suggested.

EVALUATING THE EVALUATORS
AND THE EVALUATION PROGRAM

Three major elements are involved in this procedure: (1) Is the evaluator consistent and fair? (2) Are the standards obtainable and reasonable? and (3) Does the evaluation methodology separate employee performance into excellent, average and poor categories?

1. *Is the evaluator consistent and fair?*

This variable may be checked by having different persons evaluate the same men as they perform identical tasks. If the evaluations, when done independently, are reasonably consistent, the evaluator has done his evaluation well. If the evaluations are inconsistent, a further study needs be made to determine whether a specific administrator is incapable of performing an acceptable evaluation; and, if he is not, he should be removed from the role of evaluator. If the evaluator is acceptable, the instruments and methodologies used may need to be reworked.

2. *Are the standards obtainable and reasonable?*

A scheme can be planned for all job categories which will allow the standards to be checked. In the case of the

LEWISTON-PORTER CENTRAL SCHOOL
Youngstown, New York

Cleaner-Maintenance Helper Evaluation Form

Name of Employee   Name of Evaluator

                                    Date of Evaluation
Area I - General Characteristics
                                    Acceptable   Unacceptable

1. Appearance   ___/   ___/

    If unacceptable, state the specifics and determine and list a

    program to correct the problem: _____

    _____

    _____

2. Ability to get along with:

        Fellow workers   ___/   ___/

        School Patrons   ___/   ___/

        Administrators   ___/   ___/

        Teachers   ___/   ___/

        Others   ___/   ___/

    If unacceptable, state the specifics and determine and list a

    program to correct the problem: _____

    _____

    _____

3. Health   ___/   ___/

    If unacceptable, state the specifics and determine and list a

    program to correct the problem: _____

    _____

    _____

Figure 8-4

	Acceptable	Unacceptable

4. Knowledge of techniques, materials $\boxed{}$ $\boxed{}$

    supplies and equipment use

    If unacceptable, state the specifics and determine and list a

    program to correct the problem: _____

    _____

    _____

5. Attendance Record $\boxed{}$ $\boxed{}$

    If unacceptable, state the specifics and determine and list a

    program to correct the problem: _____

    _____

    _____

Area II - Specific Tasks

		Excellent	Above Average	Average	Below Average	Poor
	Vacuuming	$\boxed{}$	$\boxed{}$	$\boxed{}$	$\boxed{}$	$\boxed{}$
2	Dusting	$\boxed{}$	$\boxed{}$	$\boxed{}$	$\boxed{}$	$\boxed{}$
3.	Cleaning Glass	$\boxed{}$	$\boxed{}$	$\boxed{}$	$\boxed{}$	$\boxed{}$
4	Cleaning lavatories	$\boxed{}$	$\boxed{}$	$\boxed{}$	$\boxed{}$	$\boxed{}$
5	Cleaning Chalkboards	$\boxed{}$	$\boxed{}$	$\boxed{}$	$\boxed{}$	$\boxed{}$
6	Checking doors and windows for security	$\boxed{}$	$\boxed{}$	$\boxed{}$	$\boxed{}$	$\boxed{}$
7.	Emptying wastebaskets	$\boxed{}$	$\boxed{}$	$\boxed{}$	$\boxed{}$	$\boxed{}$
8.	Checking temperature controls	$\boxed{}$	$\boxed{}$	$\boxed{}$	$\boxed{}$	$\boxed{}$
9.	Changing burned out lights	$\boxed{}$	$\boxed{}$	$\boxed{}$	$\boxed{}$	$\boxed{}$

	Excellent	Above Average	Average	Below Average	Poor
10. Cleaning blinds	☐	☐	☐	☐	☐
11. Condition cleaning carpet	☐	☐	☐	☐	☐
12. Painting areas indicated	☐	☐	☐	☐	☐
13. Repairing minor furniture and equipment repair	☐	☐	☐	☐	☐
14. Cleaning woodwork	☐	☐	☐	☐	☐
15. Performing specialized tasks requested by: teachers	☐	☐	☐	☐	☐
principal	☐	☐	☐	☐	☐
Shift Supervisor	☐	☐	☐	☐	☐
16. Others (list)	☐	☐	☐	☐	☐

The boxes checked below average or poor were checked for the following reasons: _____

_____

_____

_____

The corrective program needed is as follows: _____

_____

_____

_____

_____

Area III - Summary

    A. To be completed by evaluator:

        1. I believe that the single most strength of _____

        _____ is _____
        name of employee

        _____

Figure 8-4 (cont.)

2. I believe that the single most weakness of _____

_____ is _____
name of employee

_____

_____

3. I recommend the following courses of action be taken as

they relate to _____:
                  name of employee

  a. Recommend for promotion   /___/

  b. Recommend reassignment   /___/   _____
                                        where reassigned
  c. Recommend job retraining   /___/

  program

    (1) Specific suggestions _____

_____

_____

  d. Recommend termination   /___/

  e. Others (list)

_____

_____

Date _____   Signature of Evaluator _____

B. To be completed by employee: Yes   No

  1. I have read this evaluation   /_/   /_/

  and have had a conference with

  the evaluator.

  2. I agree with this evaluation /_/   /_/

    a. If no, with what specific

    statements, do you disagree? (list):

_____

_____

_____

_____

_____

3. I wish to be reevaluated by   ◿   ◿

another evaluator

_____   _____
Date   Signature of Employee

Figure 8-4 (cont.)

cleaner, another cleaner, who is rated "average" can be
temporarily assigned to the area in question. If the "average" cleaner can perform satisfactorily, the standards
should be retained. If he can not perform satisfactorily,
the standards should be modified.

3. *Does the evaluation discriminate among the excellent,
average, and poor employees?*

This matter may be quickly checked if there is a large
number of employees in the specific job category. If the
number of employees is small, it can be checked over a
longer period of time. In reviewing, for example, some 200
evaluations of 50 employees over a 2 year period, it is
obvious that some excellent, many average, and some poor
evaluations should be registered. If not, the evaluators and
the system of evaluation should be closely reviewed to
determine the reasons for the inability to discriminate between levels of employee performance. A total new system
may need be established.

FURTHER THOUGHTS

In establishing a system of evaluation for classified employees
some techniques, that have not been mentioned previously, need
be mentioned. The techniques of quality control, cost effectiveness analysis and cost efficiency analysis are important tools in
establishing the basis upon which evaluation is built.

1. *Quality Control*—The application of this concept to performance objectives is a very fruitful step to take prior to the
establishment of the total evaluation program. Acceptable
error margins can be established in terms of how many

letters can acceptably be retyped per 100 letters by a secretary, how much food need be thrown away because of the lack of proper levels of seasoning by a cook, how many times does a wax job on floors need be redone per 100 applications by a cleaner, and numerous other possibilities.

2. *Cost Effectiveness Analysis and Cost Efficiency Analysis*

The term *cost effectiveness* is used to determine the output received from a method based upon a standard or objective. It is the term used when outputs cannot be easily quantified in terms of dollars spent. For example, the distribution and processing of filmstrips may be done at a minimum dollar amount per 1,000 uses, but the criterion of getting them to the teachers when they are needed for instruction may not be met. In this case, a cost effectiveness study may cause a decision to buy multiple copies of the same filmstrip to be housed in each school building, or it may cause a change in the charge out time of the filmstrip to 5 days from the current 3 days.

The term *cost efficiency analysis* is applied when alternate outputs or methods can be quantified in such a way that the dollar amount expended per unit of production can be computed. Examples of use are (1) The purchasing of a diesel tractor with gang mowers rather than hand mowers for the grounds staff after a study shows that over a 3-year-period, $16,000 in wages would be saved in labor costs, or (2) An automatic collator purchased for an office staff proved a saving of 360 man hours per year at $2.75 per hour in an office staff of 10 secretaries. The collator cost $425.00. This computes as follows:

360 man hours x $2.75 per hour	=	$ 990.00
Cost of collator	=	425.00
Savings (first year)		$ 565.00

If the life expectancy of the collator is five years, it is evident that the savings are much greater than that indicated at the first years' savings.

Nine

EVALUATING THE CO-CURRICULAR STAFF AND UNIQUE, INNOVATIVE POSITIONS

The major steps in developing a program of evaluation for co-curricular and unique positions parallel each other. The process includes: (1) programming the goals, (2) detailing the procedures, (3) arriving at the techniques to be employed during the evaluation process, (4) deciding on the personnel to perform the evaluations, and (5) planning to evaluate the evaluators and the evaluation program that has been established.

Other problematic areas to be discussed within the context of this chapter include: (1) deciding on the weightings to be allotted to the variables of time spent, numbers of pupils supervised, responsibilities for schedules and equipment and the "pressure" factor, and (2) determining the evaluative variables when no prototype position or model exists.

CO-CURRICULAR POSITIONS

Programming the Goals

Initially, a great deal of time must be spent by the individuals who are responsible for the development of the evaluation system for co-curricular positions, and by those individual staff members who are to hold the positions of coach or sponsor, in the discussions of the goals of the co-curricular programs. Some goals may cut across all co-curricular programs, while other goals must be specifically developed for each class of co-curricular offering. Obviously, a football program, a marching band program, a graphics club, an auto mechanics club, an ecology club, and an endless variety of other co-curricular offerings will vary in their specific programmatic goals. Some basic assumptions, such as those listed below, will evolve. Examples of specific programmatic goals are also presented below.

General assumptions:

1. Co-curricular offerings are desirable in providing comprehensive learning experiences within the sponsorship of the local school district. Such offerings provide non-classroom experiences that cannot be duplicated in any other manner.
2. Co-curricular offerings provide a wide choice of individualized free choice experiences that are normally not present in the regular course offerings.
3. Many cognitive experiences, (in areas such as forensics and ecology), psychomotor experiences (in areas such as skiing and football), and affective experiences (in areas such as marching band, creative dance and pop art), are provided youngsters through a wide variety of co-curricular offerings.

Program goals:

Following many additional hours of planning, a listing of specific goals will evolve. It must be remembered, however, that even specific goals are, and should be, subject to change over time. A listing of specific goals for the co-curricular activity of marching band will serve as an example of the type of specific goals that need be established for each co-curricular offering. These specific goals then provide a document from which the director of marching bands can be evaluated.

Goal #1—To arrive at a division of labor that will permit the total staff assigned to marching band to produce a maximum effort with a minimum amount of duplication. This goal must consider the functions of the director, the assistant directors, the pom pom coordinator and the baton twirling corp coordinator.

Goal #2—To allow the person being evaluated and the person conducting the evaluation to realize the specific tasks and responsibilities assigned to each individual. A well-written, comprehensive job description is one tool that is helpful in the achievement of this goal.

Goal #3—To permit the employee and his immediate supervisor and/or evaluator to establish long term and interim objectives that are to be accomplished over a definite period of time. Written behavioral objectives which state the means of measurement and the minimal level of performance that is deemed acceptable will greatly assist in the achievement of this goal.

Goal #4—To provide for genuine face-to-face discussion of achievements and areas of weakness that are in need of improvement. This provision is based on the assumption that the immediate supervisor and/or evaluator will schedule a sufficient number of evaluative conferences, utilizing the observations from his visits, the job description and the agreed upon behavioral objectives, so as to assist the employee being evaluated in an individualized program designed to improve the areas of weakness that have been identified.

Detailing the Procedures

Utilizing the example category of marching band director, the procedures that would appear to be of maximum assistance are those of a written job description and the development of a written listing of performance objectives. These two documents provide the basic standards upon which the band director's evaluation can be based.

JOB DESCRIPTION

The job description that was arrived at for the marching band director of Lewiston—Porter Central School of Youngstown, New York is presented below. Other district's job descriptions may be more generalized or more specifically detailed. The Lewiston—Porter job descriptions, coupled with a listing of performance objectives, does provide a useable system of documents for the evaluation of a marching band director.

PERFORMANCE OBJECTIVES

The yearly performance objectives for the marching band director might be stated as follows. Of course, the performance objectives will change with time, with different individuals filling the assignment of marching band director, with the number of students in the marching band and with the number of assistants provided the director. Although the objectives listed are long term, the director and his immediate supervisor and/or evaluator may well wish to develop a supplemental list of interim objectives.

Objective #1—The number of students who try out for the marching band on an elective basis shall be increased by a minimum of 5% over the previous year.

Objective #2—The number of students who decide to quit the marching band after being admitted to membership will be less than 1% of the total membership.

Objective #3—A minimum of 10% of the graduating seniors who participated in marching band the previous year and who have gone on to college will try out for the univeristy's marching band. A minimum of 5% of the graduating seniors who participated in the high school marching band the previous year and who have gone directly into the world of work will attempt to join a municipal or other band unit.

Objective #4—There shall be less than 3 student behavior problems, as reported by the officials of other schools, during the current marching band season. No more than 1% of the students shall be involved in behavioral problems, and no single student shall be involved in more than a single case of student misbehavior.

Objective #5—The director shall not let the expenditures for marching band exceed 5% of the previous year's budget for that activity.

Objective #6—The marching band shall compete in two area competitions and in one State competition during the current marching band season. The marching band shall

```
┌─────────────────────────────┐
│Superintendent of Schools    │
└─────────────────────────────┘
              │
┌─────────────────────────────┐
│Assistant Superintendent     │
│    for Instruction          │
└─────────────────────────────┘
              │
┌─────────────────────────────┐
│    Building Principal        │
└─────────────────────────────┘
              │
┌─────────────────────────────┐
│Director of Marching Band    │
└─────────────────────────────┘
```

I. Qualifications

    A. Required Qualifications

        1. Shall hold a valid music teaching certificate for New
York State.

    B. Desirable Qualifications

        1. Shall possess at least five years of teaching instru-
mental music, of which three years shall include marching
band experience.

        2. Possess experience in presenting marching and maneuvering
half-time shows.

        3. Possess the ability to work with students and understand
their individual needs and problems.

        4. Has the ability to work cooperatively with individuals
and groups of individuals relevant to a marching band.

        5. Has the understanding and ability to coordinate all
phases of a marching band program   (i.e., music, marching and maneuvering, color guard, drum major, baton
twirling, pom-pom girls, and any other related area.)

II. Duties and Responsibilities

    A. General Duties and Responsibilities

        1. The Marching Band Director will be responsible to the
Senior High School principal. He will be in charge of
and coordinate all phases of the marching band, related
groups, and their instructors.

    B. Specific Duties and Responsibilities

        1. Arrange all rehearsal schedules of all pertinent groups

Figure 9-1

176

and assign duties to his assistants of related band groups.

2. Shall be responsible for starting band practice one week before the formal opening of school.

3. Shall be responsible for the performance of the band at two outside community programs, one for Youngstown, one for Lewiston, during the fall.

4. Shall have direct authority over, and responsibility for, the activities and programs of the pom-pom girls and baton twirlers.

5. Shall have ability in all financial phases of operating a marching band and related groups, and shall formulate a budget, order equipment, and secure the necessary maintenance of the equipment.

6. Shall call special rehearsals when needed.

7. Orders buses for the transportation of the band, and all related groups.

8. Evaluates performance of assistants and makes a written recommendation to the principal.

9. Works with the marching band in musical training, marching, and maneuvering.

10. Supervises and works with the instructors of the pom-pom girls and baton twirlers in integrating their programs into the complete band programs.

11. Makes suggestions to the building principal as to specific band needs.

12. Submits to the building principal an annual progress report, together with a projection of future needs.

13. Shall ride the bus and act as chaperone on all away events featuring the band.

14. Shall be responsible for the care, repair, storage and the inventory of all music, uniforms, and equipment.

15. Shall be responsible for the scheduling of tryouts for the marching band in the spring.

16. The band director will be responsible for the supervision of the band from the time school is dismissed, until practice is concluded. At all meetings, the band director is responsible for the supervision of band members from the beginning of the practice until its conclusion.

17. Provides adequate chaperones on all trips.

18. Performs in all instances in a professional manner, honoring the confidences and loyalties ascribed to and required of this position.

III. Working Conditions

As prescribed in the applicable negotiated master agreement and the policies of the Board of Education.

Figure 9-1 (cont.)

receive a minimum of one first place and one second place rating at the area level, and the marching band shall receive a minimum of a third place rating at the level of State competition.

Objective #7—No more than two conflict situations shall occur among the various members of the marching band's supervisory staff during the current marching band season.

Objective #8—At least 6 students from the marching band shall be chosen for area's all star marching band in competition with students members of marching bands from other area schools.

Objective #9—The marching band shall perform at the eight away and home football games, presenting a minimum of four different half-time performances.

Objective #10—The marching band shall volunteer its services to the local town for its Labor Day parade.

Objective #11—The marching band director shall file with the high school principal, prior to November 30th, an evaluation of each of his assistants, a proposed budget for the succeeding year, an inventory of all instruments and supplies, a schedule for the repair of instruments in need of repair, and a five year plan of future marching band needs.

Finally, the marching band director and his immediate supervisor and/or evaluator should decide upon a weighting, numerical or otherwise, to be assigned to each performance objective in order that all objectives are not deemed to be of equal importance when arriving at a finalized evaluative statement.

Arriving at the Techniques for Evaluation

Dependent upon the specific position being evaluated, techniques may vary. A track coach might be evaluated on the increase in time improvements, height improvements or distance improvements registered over the track and field season by each individual student on the track and field team. He may also be evaluated on the success, as represented by the team's win and loss record against schools of equivalent total student enrollment with a relatively equal amount of participants on their track and field teams.

A journalism club teacher may be evaluated on the ratings received in competition with other high school newspapers at a national competition. He also may be evaluated upon the number of technical errors that appear in the first issue of the student newspaper versus the number of errors identified in the last issue for the current school year.

An ecology club sponsor may be evaluated on the basis of the development of ecological study trails that are established on the school grounds, the research data gathered on the major ecological problems of the local municipality and the use of this data by municipal officials, and the number of news items dealing with the topic of ecology that the club has published in the local newspapers. He may also be evaluated on the percentage of growth in voluntary student membership within the club.

A dramatics club sponsor may be evaluated by the number and degree of difficulty of the plays produced in the current year compared to those of the preceding year. He may also be evaluated on the number of people who attend the performances put on in the current year as compared to the number attending performances in the preceding year.

Many other examples could be presented, but suffice it to say that the examples presented above are only limited examples and many additional means of evaluation need be determined. In any case, the variety of roles to be played by those employees involved in a comprehensive co-curricular program are so broad and unique that an individualized set of evaluative techniques need be agreed upon for each staff assignment.

Deciding on Personnel to Perform Evaluations

The personnel best equipped to perform the evaluations will vary as to type and number for each co-curricular assignment. One example, that of the marching band director, shall be utilized to clarify the types of logical decisions that need be made when deciding which individuals are to take part in the evaluative process.

Those individuals who might be involved in the evaluation of the marching band director and the reasons for their inclusion in the evaluative scheme are:

1. *Student marching band members*—A questionnaire could be devised that would ask whether or not the student enjoyed his participation. The student could also be asked to list the reasons why he did or did not enjoy his participation in marching band. Those students who transferred from other schools and who also participated in the marching band at other schools could be asked to compare the quality of the marching band units. The questionnaires, of course, could be answered anonymously.

2. *Lay residents and students who were not members of the marching band*—These individuals could be asked to compare the quality of the marching band's performance to those of other marching bands that they had seen perform. This could be accomplished by a simple checklist or rating scale. For the sake of practicality, the numbers involved in this type of evaluation should be merely a randomized sample.

3. *Outside experts*—Outside experts could be used to adjudicate the performance of the marching band.

4. *Co-workers*—The assistants to the marching band director

could assist in the evaluation. Their evaluations would be extremely helpful if they had also worked with other marching band directors in the past. These evaluations may best be accomplished in a face-to-face conference situation with the director.

5. *Self evaluation*—The director certainly should be able to be introspective to the degree that would permit him to determine whether or not he has achieved the personal goals that he has established prior to the beginning of the marching band season.

6. *Central office administrator*—In a school district of any significant size, the position of director of music probably exists. The inclusion of this trained musician and instructor should be mandatory in that he possesses a high degree of expertise in the field.

7. *Immediate administrative supervisor*—This individual could be the school building principal or some other administrator. In any case, he and the director of the marching band could review the marching band director's job description and the performance objectives that had previously been agreed upon for the current season. The individual will probably be the one charged with the recommendation for the appointment of a marching band director for the succeeding year; and, for that reason alone, he must become a key individual in the evaluative process.

Evaluating the Evaluators and Evaluation Program

Three major questions need be answered when evaluating the evaluators and the program of evaluation. They are: (1) Is the evaluator consistent and fair? (2) Are the standards used in evaluation obtainable and reasonable? and (3) Does the evaluation methodology discriminate among those employees who perform in an excellent, average or below average manner?

Is the evaluator consistent and fair?

The fairness and consistency may be checked by having the same employee evaluated multiple times by the same evaluator and by having two or more evaluators evaluate the same employee. In any case, if the employee is in strong disagreement with the evaluation provided, he should be given the right to insist on an evaluation by at least one additional evaluator.

If the evaluations, when conducted independently, are reasonably consistent, the evaluator is performing well. If the evaluations are inconsistent, or if a single evaluator is consistently providing low or high evaluations when compared to the evaluations of other evaluators of the identical employees, the poor evaluator should be eliminated from the evaluative process.

Are the standards obtainable and reasonable?

If the "average" employee assigned to the task can perform in an acceptable manner, the standards should be retained. If he cannot perform to the standards, the standards need be modified.

A method of checking can be developed by assigning different employees to the same assignment or tasks over time. If a series of employees are unsuccessful, the evaluative standards definitely need revision.

The above discussion of "average" performance does not indicate that an above average performance is not most desirable. The "average" performance does, however, indicate the minimal level of acceptability.

Does the evaluation discriminate among the excellent, average and below average employee?

This matter can be rapidly checked if there is a large number of employees assigned the same job responsibilities. If the number of employees is small, it can be checked over a longer period of time.

In reviewing the performance of ten or more employees over a minimum of a two-year period of time, it is common sense that some excellent, average and below average performances be registered. If not, the evaluators and the program of evaluation need be closely reviewed to determine the reasons for the inability to discriminate among levels of employee performance. A total new system may need be developed as any evaluative system must discriminate among performance levels in order to be a useful tool to a local school district.

Final Words

In the process of evaluating individuals assigned responsibilities for co-curricular activities, consideration must be given to such matters as the number of pupils supervised, the number of hours required to fulfill the obligations of the co-curricular assignment, the degree of responsibility for schedules, equipment and supplies, and the pressure factor that exists in assignments such as varsity basketball. These variables must be considered when devising the evaluative scheme for co-curricular activity assignments.

UNIQUE, INNOVATIVE POSITIONS

The major steps in the development of a program of evaluation for unique, innovative positions are identical to those presented earlier in this chapter for co-curricular positions. These steps are: (1) programming the goals, (2) detailing the procedures, (3) arriving at the techniques to be employed during the evaluative process, (4) deciding on the personnel to perform the evaluations, and (5) planning to evaluate the evaluators and the evaluative program that has been established.

The major differences between the development of an evaluative program for unique, innovative positions and all other positions in the school district are that models exist for standardized positions and the need for standardized positions has existed and has been determined at some point in the past. Unique, innovative positions are created when a new need is recognized, no existing model upon which to base the evaluative program exists, and no historical determinations have been made. Thus, even though the basic steps in the evaluative program's development are identical or similar, the difficulty of establishing an evaluative program of personnel performance for unique positions is much greater.

Because the evaluative steps have been thoroughly discussed in the section of this chapter dealing with co-curricular positions, the format of the remainder of this chapter will be modified to present only those major points in need of emphasis. The omission of the various steps in the staff evaluation process eliminates unnecessary duplication, but the reader must be reminded that each of these steps must be thoroughly investigated when developing an evaluative scheme for each category of staff position at the local school district level.

Only those major points of emphasis pertaining to unique, innovative positions will now be discussed.

Identifying the Need for the Creation
of an Unique, Innovative Position

The number of students using drugs in a local school district dramatically increases. In general, the present staff does not contain a single member who is knowledgeable about the details of drugs, the effects of drug abuse or the techniques of counseling youngsters who are users. It is also evident that the staff needs to gain knowledge about the identification of drugs and the identification and means of assisting the student user. Finally, the need for the establishment of a preventative program for student non-users is evident. The solution: the creation of the unique position of Drug Counselor.

Many classroom teachers are not receiving the assistance needed to improve their classroom performance. The administrative staff is currently given this responsibility, but the administrative staff cannot properly carry out this responsibility because they lack the necessary time, they lack the necessary degree of expertise, and they are handicapped because they are responsible for hiring, firing, tenure and other administrative decisions. This situation existed within the Lewiston-Porter Central School District when its staff decided to attempt to resolve the need by creating the position of Elementary Building Curriculum and Program Evaluation Coordinator. This position was added to each elementary school, it was given a year's pilot feasibility study, the individuals appointed were appointed on a year-to-year basis, and multiple evaluations were conducted.

Although program objectives were stated, an overview of the attempt to meet this need can be gained by studying the job description that was developed for this innovative position. Obviously, the job description and the behavioral objectives will need be modified over time.

Student unrest has increased in the school district, discipline has been more strictly enforced, and numerous charges of unfair treatment are leveled at the district's administrators. The board of education, the administrative staff and the teachers are concerned about the protection of an individual student's rights. The admin-

II - 240

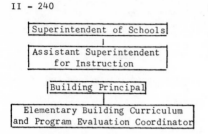

Position: Elementary Building
Curriculum and Program
Evaluation Coordinator

I. Qualifications

    A. Required Qualifications

        1. Shall hold or be eligible for an appropriate teaching
certificate for New York State.

        2. Shall have a minimum of three (3) years professional
experience in education.

    B. Desirable Qualifications

        1. Possesses a broad background of experience in education
with successful teaching experience at a level appropriate
to his assignment.

        2. Recognizes that the need for continuous evaluation of
practices in terms of children's needs, interests and
abilities is necessary in an effective instructional
program.

        3. Has ability to locate, organize, and use time, methods,
materials and information effectively.

        4. Has a knowledge of child development, learning theories
and group processes.

        5. Is tolerant of personality differences.

        6. Is concerned with the understanding of the potentials and
limitations of each teacher in order to help him attain
realistic goals.

Figure 9-2

7. Has ability to work cooperatively with each teacher and groups of teachers in the solution of problems and the implementation of innovative programs.

8. Is familiar with all facets of good instruction and current curricular developments.

9. Has good understanding of human relations and skill in public relationships.

II. Responsibilities

    A. General Duties and Responsibilities

        The Elementary Building Curriculum and Program Evaluation Coordinator is directly responsible to the building principal for the coordination and evaluation of in-class performance and matters pertaining to curriculum within the building to which he is assigned.

        The Elementary Building Curriculum and Program Evaluation Coordinator is not an administrator and does no formal evaluation of staff for tenure or for any other reasons. He is a confidant of teachers without specific feedback to the building principal regarding individual performance.

    B. Specific Duties and Responsibilities

    1. Works with classroom teachers through individual and group conferences in the selection and use of instructional materials.

    2. Works with the teaching staff in providing an enriched and sequential learning situation for each child.

    3. Assists the classroom teacher in observing individual students and making diagnosis of students who are not progressing according to their apparent potential. He

Figure 9-2 (cont.)

also assists the classroom teacher in providing remediation and service for students who need a corrective
program.

4. Assists teachers in planning, in the use of instructional
   materials and curriculum guides and in methods and
   techniques.

5. Utilizes the services of the Media Coordinator, Curriculum Coordinator and other specialists in the district
   in assisting the individual classroom teacher and the
   total staff of the building assigned.

6. Seeks opportunities to assist teachers in improving
   their planning and teaching activities and initiates
   assistance when a need is recognized but not requested by
   the individual teacher.

7. Maintains an information file of current materials and
   teaching devices.

8. Evaluates, with the classroom teacher, the instructional
   environment utilizing video tapes, interaction analysis,
   demonstration lessons, mini-lessons, simulations and other
   meaningful procedures.

9. Assists the building principal and the building teaching
   staff in the planning and implementation of desirable
   curriculum changes.

10. Arranges, with the approval of the building principal,
    opportunities for teachers to observe a lesson in another
    classroom when a need is evident.

11. Arranges demonstration lessons when a need exists.

12. Performs such other duties as may be assigned by the
    building principal.

13. Submits to the building principal an annual progress

report together with a projection of needs for five

(5) years.

14. Makes suggestions to the building principal as to building

staff in-service needs.

15. Serves as a member of the Superintendent's Instructional

Council.

16. Performs in all instances in a professional manner;

honoring the confidences and loyalties ascribed to and

required of this position.

III. Working Conditions

A. Same as a classroom teacher.

B. This is a year to year appointment recommended by the Super-

intendent of Schools and approved by the Board of Education.

Figure 9-2 (cont.)

istrators also feel that they need a go-between who can assist them in the resolution of student-body problems. Besides creating an advisory committee comprised of students, residents and staff members who are charged with the responsibility of developing a policy, to be adopted by the board of education, detailing the rights and responsibilities of students; a unique position of ombudsman was developed. The ombudsman was given the major responsibility of processing all alleged charges of biased treatment leveled at the staff by the students. A student grievance procedure, similar to that of all employee groups, was developed, and the ombudsman was given free access to all facts and to discussion with all personnel. He also was given the responsibility of recommending judgemental solutions to each allegation.

The final example to be presented deals with the initial stages of development of the very unique and innovative position of educational catalyst. The example is an actual abbreviated case study that took place in the Godwin Heights School District of Wyoming, Michigan.

EDUCATIONAL CATALYST—AN ABBREVIATED CASE STUDY

Does your school district suffer from a status quo curriculum? Do you find that negotiations have hardened your staff communication and innovative arteries? Do you find that your traditional curriculum committee structure is nonproductive? Do you find that you have an administrator, such as an assistant superintendent for instruction, who is handcuffed into system inactivity?

The above questions were asked by Godwin Heights Public Schools of Wyoming, Michigan. The answers represent one attempt to think creatively about methods of getting curriculum improvement back on the constructive, innovative and productive track. Although the position of educational catalyst became a necessity because of a breakdown of the traditional system of curriculum improvement, the position holds promise for school districts who have not been embroiled in the negative by-products of collective negotiations.

Need Becomes Clear

Near strike situations arising out of heated collective bargaining caused negative reaction towards on-going curriculum improvement. For two years the assistant superintendent asked staff members to volunteer for curriculum committee assignments—an insufficient number of staff members volunteered. An attempt was made to hire small groups to work on specific curriculum development programs in the summer months—this was largely unsuccessful. Ten one-half days were added to the master contract year, and these days were to be used for curriculum study and in-service. This procedure was nonproductive because 100% of the staff was involved and 100% of the staff was not interested in productive contribution. Finally, each building principal worked with his building staff in program improvement—this was only mildly successful as the adoption of new textbooks, the scheduling of specialists and so forth seemed to be the main thrust of activity.

The frustration mounted until it was agreed by administration to take a creative look at solving the problem. The birth of a new type of specialist took place through many hours of soul-searching discussion.

The Educational Catalyst Comes Into Being

It was decided that a position of educational catalyst should be created. The position was conceived as one of almost total flexibility with improvements being made and job tasks delineated on the basis of the first year's evaluation. The following guidelines and problems were delineated, however, prior to searching for candidates:

1. Each building should be provided with its own, full-time catalyst. To do less would limit the chance of success by dissipating the individual's energies.
2. Although the worth of such a person may well be in excess of most administrative positions his salary had to be that of a teacher, and he had to be seen as part of the teachers' association. Extra compensation was made available for summer duties and other added assignments.
3. There was no specific training or experience that could be outlined for the person who would fill this job. In fact, every catalyst hired would probably be significantly different from other catalysts.
4. Red tape and administrative control must be eliminated as much as possible. To accomplish this, it was agreed that the catalyst was independent of the building principal and the assistant superintendent for instruction. However, he had to receive the building principal's permission prior to taking teachers out of class or attempting programs that may be controversial in nature. The catalyst had the right to appeal to the superintendent in cases where he did not agree with the building principal's determination.

   Another means of circumventing the red tape dilemma was by providing each catalyst with a $500 budget to be spent in any way that he determined necessary. The sum of $500 was originally established so as to provide money for substitutes if the catalyst wished to periodically free a classroom teacher from teaching duties, if he wished to buy the staff reference materials, if he wished to provide conference or visitation opportunities for staff and many other possible expenditures. The sum remained sufficiently small, however, to keep him from "buying" the staff's participation.

5. It was agreed that each catalyst would be given complete freedom during the year's operation; but a detailed, written account of activities, expenditures, successes, failures and problems would be presented by the catalyst. This report to be followed by a two-day oral evaluation by all parties concerned.

6. It was agreed that this position would be approved on a year-to-year basis, and that the persons filling the role of catalyst would also be approved on a year-to-year basis. If a person could not creatively improve instruction, he was not to be held in that position out of false loyalty. Production was the key factor in the final decision.

7. Finally, it was agreed that, based upon experience with this innovative structure, the following questions would ultimately need be answered:
   a. What should be his job description?
   b. What should be his relationship to each category of staff and student?
   c. What should be his budget, and for what purposes should his budget be expended?
   d. How can the programs with which he becomes involved be better evaluated?
   e. How many catalysts are needed to get the job done at an acceptable level?
   f. Should he have one or two teaching periods in order that he keeps immediate contact with the students and the problems of the teaching staff, or should he not have any assigned duties?
   g. Other concerns that need be resolved?

The Job was Described, Advertised Widely and Filled:

Dictionaries usually describe a catalyst as something that speeds up or slows down a chemical reaction, but the catalyst remains unchanged. The educational catalyst was defined as a human being who would insert himself into an educational environment, cause speed up on the change process, and remove himself while the change perpetuated itself. The type of individual needed was one who possessed maturity and stability while being capable of promoting an overthrow of traditional problem solutions when the traditional solutions were ineffective. He also need be a person who could motivate others into undertaking creative endeavors. Finally, he needed to be a person who had the capacity to listen and promote the best ideas of all categories of teaching and administrative personnel while combining these ideas with those of students and thoughts of his own in such a manner that productive improvements resulted.

A FINAL WORD

Each of the unique innovative positions briefly described demonstrate attempts to meet challenging needs at the local level. Detailed behavioral objectives would need be written, and all the steps of development of a complete evaluative scheme would need be conducted. Obviously, the variables that come to play on the performance of individuals filling the unique positions need be detailed and weighted as to relative importance in order to be fair as the evaluative process becomes operational.

Ten

SUMMARY AND CONCLUSIONS

This chapter discusses the means of assisting the individual after the evaluation has been completed, discusses the state of the art of evaluation, emphasizes the most current approaches that appear to hold promise for bettering the evaluative approaches of the near future, develops a systems approach to the development of a total program of staff evaluation, and provides a check list that will be useful to the individuals held responsible for the development of a total program of staff evaluation at the local district level.

Following Up the Evaluations

Evaluation is the process of assessing the degree of performance and level of acceptability of that performance at a point in time. The most basic purpose of evaluation must be the improvement of performance. There are two important elements, however, in the improvement of performance: (1) evaluation or assessment and (2) in-service or job upgrading programs which are tailor made to assist the employee being evaluated in improving the areas that were assessed as being below the minimal level of acceptance or as being areas in need of improvement.

Many programs of evaluation make the major error of limiting the district's total evaluation scheme to the assessment

193

phase. Any program of evaluation is incomplete without the addition of an in-service or a job upgrading phase. Further, it is grossly unfair to the employee being evaluated if areas of weakness are identified and no program of assistance is provided which will enable the employee to overcome his weaknesses and improve his performance.

Eight major means of providing assistance to an employee in improving his performance are presented in the discussion which follows. The advantages and disadvantages of each method are also presented.

FORMAL COURSES—This approach may be helpful if specific knowledges or skills that are lacking have been identified. They could be offered by an university or by a commercial firm. This would be an excellent possibility if the local budget will allow the payment of fees or if credit towards salary advancement could be given the participating employee. It would also be beneficial if the course could be offered within the confines of the local district's campus. Examples of this usage could be a training course at a commercial outlet for a clerk who needs to develop skill in data processing key punching, for the maintenance man who needs to learn how to repair the new air conditioning equipment that was installed, and for the teacher who needs to improve his knowledge of the new techniques of teaching biology.

Advantages:

1. This allows a variety of experts, which are not normally present within the local district's staff, to become involved in the process of staff performance improvement.
2. The incentive of financial reward can be easily built into this approach.
3. A wide variety of course offerings can be made available at any single point in time.

Disadvantages:

1. The formality of the course approach is not always well-received by all employees.
2. The costs in terms of study hours and financial outlay may become undesirable. This is especially true of courses offered off campus and after normal working hours.

3. The control of the quality of the individual course instructor is beyond control of the local school district.
4. The control of the specific course content is beyond the control of the local school district, and the content may not be of maximum benefit to the local employee.

WORKSHOPS—This approach allows, normally, for one to zero in on a specific area of need which has been identified in advance. Workshops may be sponsored by a commercial firm, an university or college, or by the local school district. One example of a locally sponsored workshop is that offered to all library aides as they assume responsibility for non-print (tapes, filmstrips, dry mounts, and so forth) media distribution and production.

Advantages:

1. Workshops usually serve a very specific purpose which has been determined in advance.
2. Workshops are normally of relatively short duration.
3. Workshops normally actively involve the participants in the process.
4. The purposes of workshops can be rather carefully controlled by the sponsoring district.

Disadvantages:

1. It is usually difficult, because of the short duration, to provide salary incentives for workshop attendance.
2. The costs in terms of employee time and financial outlay may be a deterent to participation.

ASSIGNMENT TO ANOTHER EMPLOYEE—This approach to a buddy system has numerous possibilities. It can be a standard approach utilized with all new employees, or it can be utilized in the scheduling of an employee whose weaknesses have been identified with an employee who has unusually high performance abilities in the areas of identified weakness. An example would be the case of a cook who is capable of providing the proper portions of food without waste in a reasonable amount of time, but who does not properly season the food in such a way as the student purchasers choose to buy lunch in the school cafeteria. A one week assignment of work with a cook who is an expert at food seasoning could probably resolve the employee's problem, and the solution should also increase the sales of student lunches.

Advantages:

1. A co-worker assigned identical tasks is the individual who most likely can provide detailed assistance in the area needing improvement.
2. The cost of this approach is negligible because both employees continue to perform their tasks. The only difference is that they work closely together over the assigned time period. The only minor inconvenience that may be involved is the temporary re-assignment of two or three employees.
3. This approach can very easily be built into the program on a continuous basis for all employee groups.

Disadvantages:

1. Although the employee to whom the other employee is assigned may be able to perform the specific task in an exemplary manner, he may not be capable of imparting the knowledge or technique to another employee.
2. One employee, because of his expertise in many task areas, may lower his level of production due to his being assigned as a trainer for too many other employees.

VISITATION—A visitation to another work station involving excellent production standards can be most helpful. A cafeteria director who is to be held responsible for converting the program of food preparation within each school building to one in which the entire district's meals are prepared out of a central kitchen may identify needed staffing patterns, work flow procedures and needed equipment placement in a short period of time.

Advantages:

1. Visiting a successful station or employee provides know how and motivation.
2. Visiting a successful station proves to the employee that it can be done, and it demonstrates how the task can be acceptably performed.
3. Visitations are easily made a continous part of any

employee long term improvement program for all categories of employees.
4. Visitations are usually of moderate cost, and the loss of employee on-the-job time is minimal.

Disadvantages:

1. Visitations can provide motivational inspiration and rapid recovery of information, but they do not give the employee great detail or provide him with the opportunity to perform himself.
2. Visitations may take numerous employees away from their job assignments for various lengths of time.
3. Money will have to be provided in the budget for substitute employees, travel expenses and the costs of meals and lodgings when the visitations take place out of the local district.

DEMONSTRATIONS AND SIMULATIONS—The assignment of an employee to another who is capable of demonstrating the proper way to perform the task, as well as one having the capability of evaluating the simulated performance of the employee assigned to the learning experience, is a very helpful method of rapid employee performance improvement. An example case might be that of an art teacher who is having difficulty in instructing students in the area of ceramics. The employee-instructor could demonstrate the appropriate techniques to the employee-learner. The employee-learner could then be provided with small assignments that would simulate the knowledges and skills needed to perform the total task. The employee-instructor could assist the employee-learner in an immediate evaluation of the simulated task completed, and repeated short term simulations could be continued until the employee-learner achieves an acceptable level of performance.

Advantages:

1. This method provides quality examples and near immediate evaluation.
2. Almost immediate reinforcement of the employee-learner is provided.
3. The one-to-one relationship between instructor and learner

provides a positive and individualized approach to performance improvement.

Disadvantages:

1. Both the employee-instructor and the employee-learner may have to be released from their basic job assignments for a period of time.
2. The cost of substitute workers may prove too great.
3. If broad based training or re-training is necessary, this may not be the most efficient method available.

VIDEO TAPINGS AND ASSIGNED SUPERVISOR—This method has the same basic advantages and disadvantages, and it serves the same basic purposes, as that of demonstrations and simulations. It has one major advantage and one major disadvantage over and above those mentioned for demonstrations and simulations. The additional advantage is that the video tape can be stored for multiple playback, and the video tape can visually demonstrate historical performance improvement. The additional disadvantage is the cost of video tape equipment, video tape supplies, and the released time for the employee doing the video taping.

ASSIGNMENT TO A PERFORMANCE TEAM—A valid means of providing individualized job upgrading is the assignment of the employee who needs to improve his performance to a hand-picked team of co-workers. A good example of usage of this technique would be that of an experienced teacher who has been assigned to a self-contained classroom situation for 15 years being assigned for the subsequent year to an open space building that utilizes a media saturated and individualized instruction approach. By assigning this teacher to a team leader, two team teachers, specializing in communications skills, and four aides for a one year period, he will receive detailed, in-depth job upgrading experiences and assignments that are continually planned with the help of all other employees involved in the specific learning environment.

Advantages:

1. Numerous co-workers are available to give day-to-day assistance and supervision.

2. Additional costs are eliminated by assignment to an actual position that needs be filled.
3. The upgrading experiences are tailor-made to the employee's needs, and they are completely within the control of the local district.
4. Daily and immediate feedback and evaluation are built into the process.

Disadvantages:

1. Unless vacancies exist, the placement of the employees needing assistance may have to be postponed beyond the most opportune time for such placement.
2. If the employee assigned has major weaknesses, too much time may be required of the helping employees. In turn, the performance of the helping employees may be hampered, or the helping employees may suffer from an assignment overload.

CONFERENCES—This technique may be used to advantage in any program of employee in-service and job upgrading. Examples include the business manager who needs to acquire knowledge of the PPBS (Planning, Programming, Budgeting System) technique, or the account clerk who needs to understand the programming of accounts for data processing retrieval.

Advantages:

1. Across the country, the number and topics of conferences are almost limitless.
2. Conferences are usually of short duration, and a variety of topics and displays are usually available.
3. The number of experts that are normally available at a conference could never be assembled by a local district.

Disadvantages:

1. The cost, in terms of budgetary outlays and in terms of loss of on-the-job staff time, may limit the feasibility of utilizing this method.
2. Conferences normally cannot provide long-term or in-depth assistance.

If the district's planning committee utilizes a combination of the approaches mentioned above, it will provide the maximum amount of assistance to the employees in need of help. Each district should plan to use those techniques that prove to be successful in assisting the local staff members in approving their performances. The techniques decided upon should be those best suited to the needs that have been identified at the local school district level.

Evaluation—Present and Future

Research indicates that the present problems that are identifiable in most schemes of staff evaluation are those of: (1) the inconsistency of the same rater over time and of agreement among multiple raters or evaluators, (2) the lack of a sufficient degree of validity and/or reliability in the opinionnaires, rating scales, anecdotal records, and other tools currently used in staff evaluations, (3) the lack of clear cut definitions of what the performance should be, and of the level of performance that is necessary to achieve acceptability, and (4) the lack of reliance on the measurement of "outcomes" of performance.

The answers for those who are interested in staff evaluations are not those of eliminating any attempts at evaluations or of putting all of the developmental eggs into the improvement of the traditional tools of evaluation. The future answers to improvement lie in the improvement of the traditional tools of evaluation in combination with the development of new techniques and tools. Some of the more recent developments that seem to hold promise for the future are:

1. Recorded performances—both video and audio
2. PERT and CPM (Program Evaluation Review Technique and Critical Path Method) approaches to long term development
3. Behavioral performance objectives
4. New classroom observation techniques such as those discussed by Simon and Boyer[1]
5. Systems approaches to planning

---

[1]Simon, Anita and Boyer, E. Gil. *Mirrors for Behavior.* Philadelphia, Penn.: Research for Better Schools, Inc., January, 1968.

All of the five techniques and tools mentioned above have been previously discussed with the exception of the concept of a systems approach to the planning of a total program of staff evaluation. The systems approach to total planning is a little used approach, and it holds a great deal of promise when one is attempting a broad based overview.

A total systems design for staff evaluation must consist of the elements of: (1) input, (2) analysis of input, (3) decision making, (4) implementation or operationalization, (5) output, (6) analysis of output, and (7) recycling. This system could be diagramed as shown in Figure 10-1.

AN EVALUATION SYSTEM APPROACH

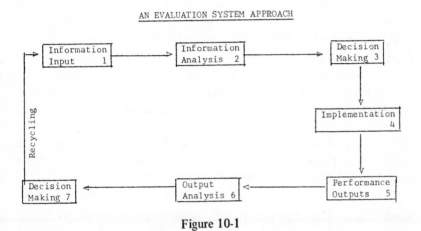

Figure 10-1

A discussion of each element in the systems design will prove beneficial at this point. It must be remembered, however, that all elements must be completed in order to build the total system. Sub systems utilizing this same model could be built in for each employee group (teachers, administrators, cafeteria workers, bus drivers, clerical workers, cleaners, and so forth). Sub systems could also be built for various buildings, or for elementary, junior high or senior high levels. Actually, sub systems could be constructed for whatever purposes seem reasonable at the local school district level.

1. *Information input component*—this is the data bank component. It could be organized in such a way that a group of staff

members could be assigned responsibility for data collection once the decision making component determines which data are needed. In the case of teachers this could be the principal of each building and the teachers assigned as evaluators. In the sub systems it could involve a combination of various supervisors and catagories of employees. It could also make use of students, residents and others.

2. *Information analysis component*—this component undertakes the responsibility for providing the data collected in a format of standards, statistics, charts and so forth as decided upon by the decision making component. This component could be the district's personnel office, it could be the computer center staff, it could be a hired group of researchers, or it could consist of a committee of selected staff members and other categories of persons.

3. *Decision making component*— undoubtedly this most important component should basically consist of representatives of each category of employee, representatives of building level and central office administration and representatives of the policy making board. This basic group could be supplemented with participants from the student body, the residents of the community and outside experts. Based upon the available data collected and analyzed, this component shall make all decisions as to time schedule, techniques of evaluation, purposes of evaluation, persons to do the evaluations and all other decisions necessary to make the program completely operational.

4. *Implementation component*—this is the component that operates the program of evaluation once all decisions have been made as to the type of staff evaluation program that is to become operational. In case of the buildings and grounds sub system this component could well consist of the superintendent of buildings and grounds, the shift supervisors, the head custodians and two employee representatives from each school building.

5. *Performance output component*—once the program has been decided upon, the program has been placed into operation, the performance standards established, and the work performed, this component takes responsibility for the quantification of performance outputs. That is, this group determines how many behavioral objectives were achieved and how many units of work

were produced in a given time period by each employee and by each group of employees. This function could be assigned to the personnel office, the administrative and supervisory staff, an outside firm or some combination of employees and administrators.

6. *Output analysis component*—this component undertakes the task of placing the quantified data in a useful form for the decision making component. This could be a function of the same group or office that functions as the information input analysis component.

7. *Decision making component*—this could be identical to the decision making component that precedes the information stage component, or it could be a separate decision making group that would serve as a check and balance system for the original decision making component. In any case, this component need be made up of a representative group of employees, administrators and policy makers. It could very well seek to include students, outside experts, residents and others in its membership.

Recycling—this is a phase of the total district's operation in the area of staff evaluation. It is an automatic process which follows the decisions made by the final decision making component. It is the elimination, addition and modification phase of the evaluative process.

A very simplified operational systems scheme for a local school district could be established as follows:

1. Information input component—each building principal, cafeteria manager, business office manager, supervisor of buildings and grounds, bus manager, and so forth.
2. Information output component—personnel director and data processing component that was hired.
3. Decision making component—a group of two employees from each employee group, the union president and vice president, an elementary principal, a secondary principal, the personnel director, the business manager, the superintendent of buildings and grounds, the assistant superintendent for instruction, the superintendent of schools, four students, eight residents, two board of education members and one hired outside expert.

4. Implementation component—evaluation team members and every person to be utilized as an evaluator.
5. Performance output component—the immediate administrative supervisors and one staff member for each staff category in each school building.
6. Output analysis component—an outside expert analyst and the director of personnel services and the computer center manager.
7. Second decision making component—this could be the same structure as the initial decision making component, or it could be a parallel group.

The remainder of this chapter will be devoted to a summary of the entire contents of this book. The summary will be presented in a checklist format that should prove to be a useful tool to the reader who is being held responsible for the development of a total staff evaluation program for his local school district.

TOTAL EVALUATION PROGRAM CHECKLIST

Directions: Place an "X" in the appropriate column.

Accomplished   Not Accomplished

1. The pre-planning stage has been completed by:

    1.1 Organizing a planning group that includes repre-
    sentatives of all employee groups, building level
    administrators, central office administrators,
    the student body, the residents of the local
    community, outside experts, or a combination of
    these categories. The advantages and disadvan-
    tages of each category has been determined.

    1.2 Developing a written listing of the duties and
    responsibilities of the planning committee.

    1.3 Establishing a continuous system of communication
    in order that all employees are informed during
    the developmental stage. The channels of communi-
    cation are designed to provide a two-way flow of
    communication. The committee meetings are open
    to visitors, the minutes of meetings are widely
    distributed, and a plan for soliciting total
    employee attitudes and suggestions has been devel-
    oped.

Figure 10-2

____ ____ 2. The review stage has been completed by:

____ ____   2.1 Reviewing all current research findings on the area of staff evaluation.

____ ____   2.2 Collecting all available information on the program presently being conducted at the local school district level.

____ ____   2.3 Determining the purposes, effectiveness and level of employee acceptance of the local evaluation program that is currently being conducted.

____ ____   2.4 Collecting materials from other school districts, industrial sources and businesses that are widely known for their leadership in the field of staff evaluation.

____ ____ 3. The planning stage has been completed by:

____ ____   3.1 Stating the philosophy, objectives and/or purposes of the total staff evaluation program. The following reasons have been considered for inclusion or exclusion:

      3.1.1 Improving employee performance.

      3.1.2 Motivating employees to more closely attain their potential.

      3.1.3 Letting employees know what is expected of them.

      3.1.4 Providing input informations for numerous administrative decisions.

      3.1.5 Determining whether or not tenure is to be granted.

      3.1.6 Differentiating staff assignments.

      3.1.7 Determining merit or performance pay.

Figure 10-2 (cont.)

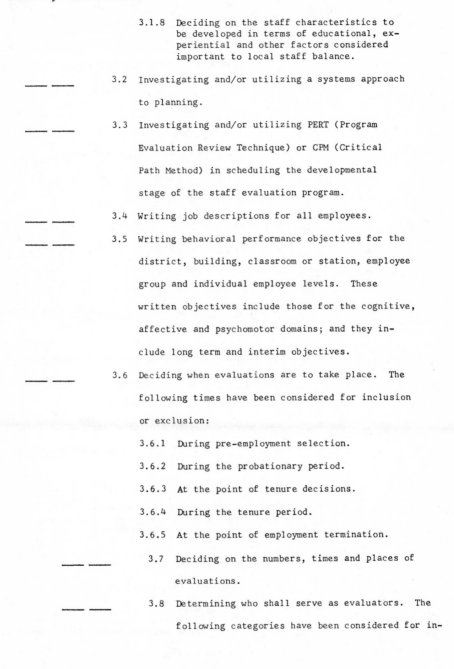

         3.1.8 Deciding on the staff characteristics to be developed in terms of educational, experiential and other factors considered important to local staff balance.

3.2 Investigating and/or utilizing a systems approach to planning.

3.3 Investigating and/or utilizing PERT (Program Evaluation Review Technique) or CPM (Critical Path Method) in scheduling the developmental stage of the staff evaluation program.

3.4 Writing job descriptions for all employees.

3.5 Writing behavioral performance objectives for the district, building, classroom or station, employee group and individual employee levels. These written objectives include those for the cognitive, affective and psychomotor domains; and they include long term and interim objectives.

3.6 Deciding when evaluations are to take place. The following times have been considered for inclusion or exclusion:

    3.6.1 During pre-employment selection.

    3.6.2 During the probationary period.

    3.6.3 At the point of tenure decisions.

    3.6.4 During the tenure period.

    3.6.5 At the point of employment termination.

    3.7 Deciding on the numbers, times and places of evaluations.

    3.8 Determining who shall serve as evaluators. The following categories have been considered for inclusion or exclusion:

3.8.1 Self evaluation.

3.8.2 Peers within the employee's group.

3.8.3 Students.

3.8.4 Lay residents.

3.8.5 Outside paid consultants.

3.8.6 Immediate administrative supervisors.

3.8.7 Central office administrators.

3.8.8 Combinations of the above categories.

3.9 Determining what is to be evaluated. Consideration
has been given to evaluation by work standards
that have been developed and to specific behavioral
objectives that have been developed by the individual employee and the immediate administrative
supervisor and/or evaluator.

3.10 Deciding on the techniques and tools to be used
in conducting the evaluations. The advantages
of each have been determined. The following
have been considered for inclusion or exclusion:

3.10.1 Cost-benefit and cost-effectiveness analy-
ses.

3.10.2 Simulations.

3.10.3 Video and audio recordings.

3.10.4 Classroom interaction observational
techniques.

3.10.5 Questionnaires.

3.10.6 Anecdotal records.

3.10.7 Rating scales.

3.10.8 Performance compared to job descriptions.

3.10.9 Performance compared to stated behavioral
objectives.

Figure 10-2 (cont.)

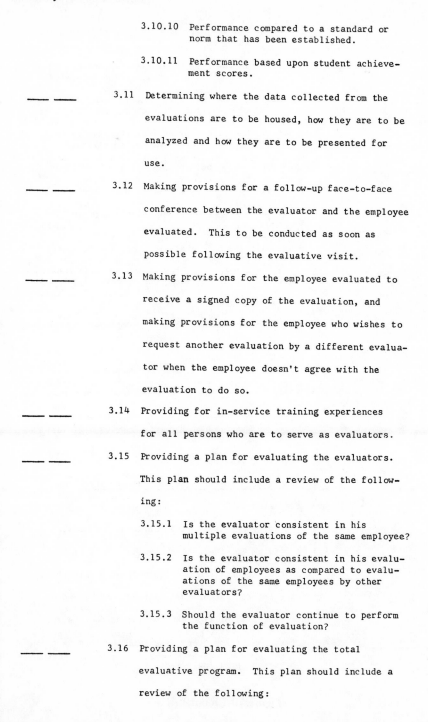

        3.10.10 Performance compared to a standard or norm that has been established.

        3.10.11 Performance based upon student achievement scores.

3.11 Determining where the data collected from the evaluations are to be housed, how they are to be analyzed and how they are to be presented for use.

3.12 Making provisions for a follow-up face-to-face conference between the evaluator and the employee evaluated. This to be conducted as soon as possible following the evaluative visit.

3.13 Making provisions for the employee evaluated to receive a signed copy of the evaluation, and making provisions for the employee who wishes to request another evaluation by a different evaluator when the employee doesn't agree with the evaluation to do so.

3.14 Providing for in-service training experiences for all persons who are to serve as evaluators.

3.15 Providing a plan for evaluating the evaluators. This plan should include a review of the following:

        3.15.1 Is the evaluator consistent in his multiple evaluations of the same employee?

        3.15.2 Is the evaluator consistent in his evaluation of employees as compared to evaluations of the same employees by other evaluators?

        3.15.3 Should the evaluator continue to perform the function of evaluation?

3.16 Providing a plan for evaluating the total evaluative program. This plan should include a review of the following:

       3.16.1 How well are the purposes of evaluation
          being met?

       3.16.2 Is the plan discriminating among the
          various levels of performance quality?

       3.16.3 Is the plan efficient in terms of employee
          time and the district's cost?

       3.16.4 Do the employees feel the plan is fair,
          equitable, reasonable and helpful?

____ ____ 3.17 Determining methods of assisting the employees

      to improve their performances after the evaluations

      have been completed. The following procedures

      have been reviewed for possible inclusion or

      exclusion:

       3.17.1 Formal university or commercially

          sponsored courses.

       3.17.2 Assignment to another employee.

       3.17.3 Visitations.

       3.17.4 Demonstrations and simulations.

       3.17.5 Video tapings and assigned supervisor.

       3.17.6 Assignment to a performance team.

       3.17.7 Conferences.

       3.17.8 Workshops.

____ ____ 4. The first year's operational feasibility stage has

    been completed by:

____ ____ 4.1 Providing for weekly informational feedback.

____ ____ 4.1 Providing for in-process changes. That is, mean-

     ingful changes are made quickly as difficulties

     are located rather than waiting for the end of

     of the feasibility year to make needed changes.

____ ____ 4.3 Operationalizing every aspect of the program

     decisions previously made.

Figure 10-2 (cont.)

____ ____ 5. The evaluation stage has been completed by:

____ ____   5.1 Collecting all necessary data.

____ ____   5.2 Evaluating all data that has been collected.

____ ____   5.3 Reviewing all evaluated data.

____ ____   5.4 Eliminating, adding and modifying staff evaluation
           program elements based upon decisions made after
           the evaluation review.

____ ____ 6. The long-term operational stage has been completed by:

____ ____   6.1 Making long-term decisions following the evalua-
           tion stage.

____ ____   6.2 Providing long-term answers to the following
           questions:

           6.2.1 Why is evaluation to take place?

           6.2.2 What is to be evaluated?

           6.2.3 Who is to evaluate and who is to be
                 evaluated?

           6.2.4 When are evaluations to take place?

           6.2.5 Where are evaluations to be conducted?

           6.2.6 How are evaluations to be conducted?

           6.2.7 What happens to improve performance
                 after evaluations have been completed?

____ ____ 7. The re-cycling stage has been completed by:

____ ____   7.1 Insisting on built-in procedures for annual
           evaluations of evaluators and for evaluating the
           total program of staff evaluation.

____ ____   7.2 Insisting on the creation of a monitoring and
           decision making committee which is assigned the
           responsibility for operationalizing modifications
           to the staff evaluation program as needed changes
           are identified.

INDEX